WALKING
WITH THE
GOD WHO
CARES

WALKING
WITH THE
GOD WHO
CARES

CATHERINE MARTIN

HARVEST HOUSE PUBLISHERS

EUGENE, OREGON

WALKING WITH THE GOD WHO CARES
Copyright © 2007 by Catherine Martin
Published by Harvest House Publishers
Eugene, Oregon 97402

Library of Congress Cataloging-in-Publication Data
Martin, Catherine, 1956–
  Walking with the God who cares / Catherine Martin.
      p. cm.
  ISBN-13: 978-0-7369-1754-4 (pbk.)
  ISBN-10: 0-7369-1754-3
  1. Spirituality.   2. Devotional literature.   I. Title.
  BV4501.3.M2755 2007
  248.4—dc22

                                                                2007002502

Printed in the United States of America

          07   08   09   10   11   12   13   14   / VP-SK /   10   9   8   7   6   5   4   3   2

Dedicated to my precious mother,
Elizabeth LaRue Stuter Snyder,
who has taught me by her words and her life
what it means to live with hope
in the most adverse of circumstances.
Mother, I have learned from you
to praise the Lord
in the shadow of the night
as well as in the light of the day.
You will always be my great example in life.

You must worship Christ as Lord of your life.
And if someone asks about your Christian hope,
always be ready to explain it.

1 Peter 3:15 nlt

Because of his glory and excellence,
he has given us great and precious promises.
These are the promises that enable you to
share his divine nature and escape the world's
corruption caused by human desires.

2 Peter 1:4 nlt

Let us hold tightly without wavering
to the hope we affirm, for God can
be trusted to keep his promise.

Hebrews 10:23 nlt

CONTENTS

Week Five—Hope in What He Says

FOREWORD
BY EMILIE BARNES

"My hope is built on nothing less than Jesus' blood and righteousness."

Catherine Martin, whom I have personally known for several years, captures this theme throughout this book. She brings to her writing the extra energy she has in her life. She radiates her excitement from Jesus the moment you meet her. Her bright smile and her sweet spirit come from the hope that Scripture gives us in everyday life. She isn't living in an ivory tower. Her 30-day journey is designed to help you come face-to-face with God the Father, God the Son, and God the Holy Spirit.

As founder and president of Quiet Time Ministries and director of Women's Ministries at Southwest Community Church in Indian Wells, California, Catherine has traveled many valleys in her lifetime. She isn't speaking from theological theory only but also from experiences she has lived.

This journey of infusing hope into one's everyday walk with the Lord is designed for personal use or large or small group study. The back of the book has four appendixes that will give group leaders the tools they need to facilitate group study, sharing, and prayer.

Catherine shares with her readers how she has known deep suffering, but these pains have challenged her to be the woman she is today. Often she wanted to escape, but she didn't. In those dark days she threw herself at the mercy of God, not knowing if she could endure. Through the trials, God showed her that there is hope in trusting God in all He says He will do for believers. She admits that all of this suffering has made her a warrior for the kingdom.

In a marvelous way, she walks you through 30 days of hope-building studies. You might feel as if you have little hope, but as Catherine guides you through Scripture, you will experience great assurance and the hope that is found only in Jesus.

At the Place of the Sea

by Annie Johnson Flint

Have you come to the Red Sea place in your life,
Where, in spite of all you can do,
There is no way out, there is no back,
There is no other way but through?
Then wait on the Lord with a trust serene
Till the night of your fear is gone;
He will send the wind, He will heap the floods,
When He says to your soul, "Go on."

And His hand will lead you through—clear through—
Ere the watery walls roll down,
No foe can reach you, no wave can touch,
No mightiest sea can drown;
The tossing billows may rear their crests,
Their foam at your feet may break,
But over their bed you shall walk dry shod
In the path that your Lord will make.

In the morning watch, 'neath the lifted cloud,
You shall see but the Lord alone,
When He leads you forth from the place of the sea
To a land that you have not known;
And your fears shall pass as your foes have passed,
You shall be no more afraid;
You shall sing His praise in a better place,
A place that His hand has made.

INTRODUCTION

Ill of life is a journey, a pilgrimage of the heart from the things of this world to the heart of God Himself. God tells a unique story through each journey. He is the Master Artist, painting a masterpiece with color and texture on the canvas of our lives, bringing glory to Him for the world to see. When the canvas allows the Master Artist to paint the picture using His oils, His tools, and His genius, He creates something amazing and wonderful that has never been seen before. He puts that masterpiece on display in galleries of His own choice to influence others so they will allow Him to work on the canvas of their lives as well.

My mother gave me a love for books and reading at a very young age. I was soon drawn to biographies and began reading stories of people who triumphed in the tragedies of life. I was drawn to the overcomers, and I sought to discover their secrets.

Suffering is an essential part of the foundation upon which all of life rises or falls. I remember reading the story of Jim Elliot, who was martyred for his faith in Christ. I read his journal entries in *The Shadow of the Almighty* and was profoundly moved by the depth of his relationship with the Lord. The lives of Corrie ten Boom and Darlene Deibler Rose took me to a new place in my own thinking. When I read their stories, and especially about their suffering, I was devastated. I sobbed and sobbed as I realized what they had endured during World War II. I was captivated by their ability to persevere through their trials; their victories in the midst of adversity made a lasting impression on me. I have never forgotten their stories. It was a wake-up call for me to realize that people can go through absolutely devastating circumstances and stand firm in their faith. Little did I know that I too would face pain and suffering. I had read about Corrie and Darlene for a reason. The Lord wanted me to see their examples so I would not give up as I ran my own race.

I confess I have known deep suffering. The pain of sorrows I have endured has challenged me to the core of my being. Sometimes I wished to escape and could not. Sometimes I felt so desperate, I wanted to give in to despair. In those dark times, I have thrown myself at the mercy of God, not knowing if I could endure. Sometimes I have cried out to the Lord, "Enough!" And then, in other times, I have marched resolutely on. Through my own suffering I have had to make a decision: Will I just give up, or will I go on with the Lord? In my journey through my own Red Sea, God has forged a path where no path existed at all, and He has shown me magnificent views at unexpected places along the way. The Lord has held me strong. He has made me into a warrior for the kingdom.

And He is in the process of making me and all who will stay on His path radical disciples for His kingdom. We are radical because we will stay the course regardless of the cost. Radical disciples for the kingdom, recklessly abandoned to the will of God, will face obstacles and adversity. You become a radical disciple when you surrender to the Lord in your circumstance, grab hold of His promises in His Word, and run your race with endurance, fixing your eyes on Jesus every step of the way. This book will help you stay the course, learn to surrender to God, and become a radical disciple for His kingdom. It speaks of hope in the face of the deepest darknesses of life. God has plenty to say in His Word about finding hope when you see no earthly reason to hope. That is the great secret. "Blessed be the God and Father of our Lord Jesus Christ, who according to His great mercy has caused us to be born again *to a living hope* through the resurrection of Jesus Christ from the dead" (1 Peter 1:3).

This is not meant to be a psychological treatise on specific kinds of sufferings—plenty of how-to books are available for dealing with every kind of personal loss and struggle. These books can help you as you walk through your darkness. But somewhere along the way, in the darkness, you must reach the heart of the eternal perspective—God's view—and connect with Him in the depth of your pain so you can stay the course with your Lord. Nothing is like the power of God's Word in adversity. The promises in the Word of God will help you stay your course with your Lord. The canvas must remain on the easel and allow the Master Artist to paint His masterpiece and display it in His gallery for His glory. This is the purpose and goal of this book.

If you had the opportunity to take the 30-day journey of *Six Secrets to a Powerful Quiet Time* (Harvest House Publishers, 2005), you discovered the joy of radical intimacy with God through quiet time with Him. You learned the P.R.A.Y.E.R. Quiet Time Plan:

P repare Your Heart

R ead and Study God's Word

A dore God in Prayer

Y ield Yourself to God

E njoy His Presence

R est in His Love

And you were encouraged to use a Quiet Time Notebook in your quiet time to help you on your journey to intimacy with God. Then, in the 30-day journey of *Knowing and Loving the Bible* (Harvest House Publishers, 2007), we continued the journey, transforming Bible reading and study into an act of love, bringing you face-to-face with God and His truth for your life. We learned how to devotionally study the Word of God. *Walking with the God Who Cares* is the journey of experiencing God's promises in the midst of life's circumstances. It demonstrates a theology of hope from God's eternal perspective.

HOW TO USE *WALKING WITH THE GOD WHO CARES*

Each week you will *read, respond,* and *experience:*

Read. In each day's reading, interact with the ideas by underlining what is significant to you and writing your comments in the margins. This book will encourage you to learn, grow, and develop a great love for God's promises in the Bible. Please mark it up and make it yours! You will also want to keep your Bible close by to look up those verses that mean the most to you on this 30-day journey.

Respond. To help you think through and apply all that I have written here, I included a devotional response section at the end of each day. You'll find a key verse to meditate on and memorize. For further thought, I have provided questions for you to consider. Finally, you'll find a place for you to express your thoughts and respond to what you have read. This is your opportunity to dialogue with God about walking with Him, finding hope, and trusting His promises in His Word.

Experience. For practical application, each week ends with a complete quiet time that emphasizes the principles you will have learned in that section. Use the blank Notes page to record what you learn from the companion DVD to this book.

Share your journey. Read what others are learning on their journey through this book and share your own insights with others throughout the world, posting your thoughts on the Quiet Time Ministries discussion board at www.quiettimecafe.com.

SUGGESTED APPROACHES FOR
WALKING WITH THE GOD WHO CARES

You can benefit from this book in several ways:

Sequentially. You may want to read the book a day at a time and implement the principles before moving to the next chapter.

Topically. You may have specific topics of interest to you. If that is the case, you can look at the table of contents and focus on those topics.

Devotionally. You may choose to read this book over 30 days. The days are divided into five sections so you can take five weeks to read and think about hope and the promises of God. It can be a 30-day adventure!

SUGGESTED SETTINGS FOR
WALKING WITH THE GOD WHO CARES

Personal and private. This is the kind of book you can read again and again. It will encourage you to draw near to God, especially if you are in a season where you have lost a habit of time with your Lord in His Word or you need to shake up your quiet time because it has become lackluster and routine. You might even want to spend some extended time with this book in a beautiful setting to revive and refresh your relationship with the Lord. It's a retreat in a book!

Small groups. I encourage you to travel on this 30-day journey with some friends. What a joy it is to share what you are learning with others who also love the Lord. You can use the questions at the end of each day for your discussion together. Appendix 1 contains additional discussion questions. This book is perfect for Sunday school classes, Bible study groups, church congregations, or your family devotions.

Ministry revival campaign. You may also desire to use this book as a 30-day intensive campaign to teach, revive, and inspire those in your ministry in the area of hope, suffering, and the promises of God. A campaign like this will help your ministry grow as new small groups are formed. Included in appendix 1 are weekly discussion questions for small groups. Six accompanying messages on DVD are available from Quiet Time Ministries, covering the introductory week through week 5. For more information on using this book as a spiritual growth campaign for your group, go to www.30dayjourney.com or www.thegod whocares.com.

Now let's embark on our journey! This book is my conversation with you about walking with God and finding hope even when there is no earthly reason to hope. Peter says, "If someone asks about your Christian hope, always be ready to explain it" (1 Peter 3:15 NLT). This is my explanation for the hope in Christ that He has given to me. It is my challenge to you to touch heaven when tested by fire and to hold on to the hem of His garments when your faith is tried by adversity. I would not have you gaze longingly at the land that so many others have enjoyed—I want you to go through the gate and enter into that wondrous land of a living hope found in the matchless promises of God Himself. May God richly bless you on this journey.

HOPE WHEN
THERE IS NO HOPE

Days 1-6

HOPE FOR MY DEEPEST DARKNESS

*Blessed be the God and Father of our
Lord Jesus Christ, who according to
His great mercy has caused us to be
born again to a living hope through the
resurrection of Jesus Christ from the dead.*

1 PETER 1:3

Y ou have a living hope that can withstand the storms of life regardless of how devastating the thunder or dark the clouds. Peter said, "Blessed be the God and Father of our Lord Jesus Christ, who according to His great mercy has caused us to be born again to a living hope through the resurrection of Jesus Christ from the dead" (1 Peter 1:3). Real Christian hope, a blessing of our salvation, is always alive and never dies. The Greek Word for "living," *zao*, implies that our hope is enduring. Those who know Christ can never say they have lost their hope or that there is no hope. Real hope cannot be lost any more than God can be lost. Hope serves as the anchor for your soul. The writer of Hebrews confirms, "This hope we have as an anchor of the soul, a hope both sure and steadfast" (Hebrews 6:19). Oh, how we need this anchor, especially when faced with the deepest darkness of our lives—what some have called the dark night of the soul.

In September 1944, when Corrie ten Boom and her sister, Betsie, first saw the gray barracks surrounded by concrete walls, they gasped in horror, "Ravensbruck." It was the notorious women's death camp where 96,000 women died during World War II. Corrie reached for the small Bible hanging from a string around her neck and hidden from view under her clothing. Once in the processing barracks, Corrie saw that at the head of the line, each woman had to strip off every scrap of clothes. How could she hide her Bible? As a security guard walked by, Corrie begged him to show her the toilets. Slipping out of line, Corrie and Betsie went into the shower room, where she hid her Bible behind a pile of old wooden benches. Corrie describes it this way: "And so it was that when we were herded into that room ten minutes later; we were not poor, but rich—rich in the care of Him who was God even of Ravensbruck."[1] After the showers, once she put on the prison dress, the Bible bulged under the thin fabric. Up ahead, the prison guards were checking every prisoner as they passed through the doorway to go to their prison cells. Corrie prayed that somehow God would shield her with His angels. And He did. The woman ahead of her was searched, and so was Betsie, who was behind her. But the guards did not touch Corrie or even look at her. During another search, again the Bible was preserved to help carry the women through the hell of Ravensbruck.

Before long Corrie and Betsie were holding secret Bible studies. God used His Word to hold Corrie and Betsie and hundreds of other women near to His heart. Barracks 28 became known as "the crazy place, where they hope"—a witness to the entire camp. The guards were trained in every kind of human cruelty, yet a much greater power was at work, and the result was hope. The Bible, the Word of God, will give you the kind of hope that can withstand even a deep darkness like the one at Ravensbruck concentration camp. Corrie and Betsie ten Boom's hope was in the unseen realities in the Word of God. God's Word did not sit on a shelf or even on a page—no, it lived in their hearts.

The work of God's Word in your life is completely independent of any outward circumstance. Paul said, "For whatever was written in earlier times was written for our instruction, so that through perseverance and the encouragement of the Scriptures we might have hope" (Romans 15:4). That Greek word for "encouragement" is *paraklesis* and means comfort. It means that the Word of God comforts you and stands by you in your heart. It works in the area no man can touch—the heart. And what is the result? According to Paul in Romans 15:4, the result is *hope.*

Hope is the crowning glory of every child of God, the distinguishing mark of a Christian. It is why a suffering Christian shines as a light in the world. Only one who knows Christ and is born again can experience true biblical hope. Paul makes this clear in Ephesians 2:12 when he states that those who are separate from Christ have no hope and are "without God in the world." There is a form of hope known to the world that is nothing more than a querulous wishing that something will or will not happen. And in the end, the result is that what is hoped for may or may not happen. That is not real hope. It is human desire, wanting what we do not have or trying to get rid of something we do have.

The Greek word for "hope" in the Bible is *elpis* and points to a confident expectation. And because this kind of hope is a living hope, no circumstance can extinguish it. Only through the new birth and the sanctifying work of the Holy Spirit can a person experience this hope (1 Peter 1:2-3). In Kenneth Wuest's *Word Studies in the Greek New Testament,* he describes the Christian hope:

> [It is an] optimism that looks for the best and not for the worst, that always sees the silver lining on every cloud. By the power of the same Holy Spirit, he is able to exert his will in putting out of his mind those things that would impede its free action. Thus, the Christian has the privilege of enjoying the wholesome mental atmosphere called *Christian optimism and a carefree mind,* not a mind devoid of an appreciation of the seriousness of life and its responsibilities, but a mind not crippled and frozen by worry, fear, and their related mental attitudes.[2]

For this reason, I like to think of hope using this acrostic: **H**olding **O**n with **P**atient **E**xpectation.

The Bible is filled with messages of hope! In the Word of God, you learn that your hope is in God and in His promises (Acts 24:15; 26:6). You believe in hope (Romans 4:18), rejoice in hope (Romans 5:2), and eagerly wait in hope (Galatians 5:5). Hope makes you bold (2 Corinthians 3:12) and enables you to draw near to God (Hebrews 7:19). The Christian has the privilege of hoping for things both present and future: comfort in affliction (2 Corinthians 1:3-4), deliverance from fear (Psalm 34:4), the presence of God (Isaiah 41:10), the power of God (Acts 1:8), forgiveness of sin (1 John 1:9), answer to prayer (Jeremiah 33:3), peace (Philippians 4:6-7), strength in all things (Philippians 4:13), rest for our souls (Matthew 11:28-30), victory in adversity (Romans 8:37), the resurrection of the dead (1 Thessalonians 4:13-14), the glory of God (Romans 5:2), righteousness (Galatians 5:5), salvation (Revelation 22:3), eternal life (Titus 1:2; 3:7), the second coming of Christ (1 John 3:2-3), and heaven (Colossians 1:5). Take time to return to this list and do a word study or a topical study. Write your insights about each verse, perhaps using the *Quiet Time Notebook.*

Corrie and Betsie ten Boom discovered that their hope could endure such an earthly hell as Ravensbruck. And they would not have known the depth of God's power or the strength of His Word had they not hoped in the promises of God through the terrible circumstances of that concentration camp and that war. Betsie told Corrie while in Ravensbruck, "We must tell people what we have learned here. We must tell them that there is no pit so deep that He is not deeper still. They will listen to us, Corrie, because we have been here."[3] When Corrie began speaking around the world as "a tramp for the Lord," she would tell anyone who would listen, "No matter how deep our darkness, He is deeper still." If Corrie knew this hope, coming out of the place she called "the deepest hell man can create," then you too can know that you have a hope that is greater than the deepest darkness you face in life.

We make our songs in the day of our gladness,
When life is all laughter and joy and delight,
When never a shadow has clouded our sunshine;
But God giveth songs in the night.

He giveth songs in the night of our sorrow,
When tears are our drink and when grief is our meat,
Till we silence our weeping and still our repining
To list to those cadences sweet.

He giveth songs in the night of affliction,
When earth has no sun and the heavens no star;
Like a comforting touch in the desolate darkness
His voice stealeth in from afar.

He giveth songs, and His music is sweeter
Than earth's greatest voices and gladdest refrains;
Our loveliest melodies shade to the minor,
But His keep their full major strains.

He giveth songs when our music is over,
When our voices falter and our tongues are mute;
When trembling hands drop from the lute and the harp-strings,
And hushed are the viol and flute.

Give us Thy songs, O Thou Maker of music!
Teach us to sing, O Thou Bringer of joy!
Till nothing can silence the notes of our triumph
And naught our rejoicing destroy.[4]

ANNIE JOHNSON FLINT

My Response

DATE:

KEY VERSE: "Blessed be the God and Father of our Lord Jesus Christ, who according to His great mercy has caused us to be born again to a living hope through the resurrection of Jesus Christ from the dead" (1 Peter 1:3).

FOR FURTHER THOUGHT: Do you know Jesus Christ? Do you have a personal relationship with Him? If not, will you make a decision even now to ask Him to come into your life? You may pray a prayer like this: *Lord Jesus, I need You. Thank You for dying on the cross for my sins. I ask You now to come into my life, forgive my sins, give me eternal life, and make me the person You want me to be, in Jesus' name. Amen.* If you prayed that prayer for the first time, you can know that Jesus is living in you and that you have been "born again to a living hope" (1 Peter 1:3). If you already know Jesus, where are you in your relationship with Him? What are you facing today? Are you in a time of darkness, a trial, perhaps even a dark night of the soul? You can know that His light is brighter than the deepest darkness. Oh, may He give you, as a result of your time with Him in His Word, hope for your hurting heart.

As you begin this 30-day journey, take some time now to talk with the Lord about where you are and what you hope to gain from your time with Him. Write a letter to Him in the space provided and watch what He does in your life over the next 30 days.

MY RESPONSE: A Letter to the Lord

WHEN GOD REMEMBERS YOU

*Thus He blotted out every living thing
that was upon the face of the land…only
Noah was left, together with those that
were with him in the ark. The water
prevailed upon the earth one hundred and
fifty days. But God remembered Noah…*

GENESIS 7:23–8:1

God will remember you in the storms of your life. "But God remembered Noah" (Genesis 8:1) is one of the most insightful phrases in the entire Bible. This is a more powerful promise than you might imagine. The Hebrew word for "remember" is *zakar* and means to pay special attention to and lavish loving care on another. This remembering goes far beyond casual acknowledgment to deep care and concern. Dr. Ronald Youngblood, in his Genesis commentary, states that "to remember someone means to express concern for him and to visit him with gracious love."[1] Always know that as God remembered Noah, so He will remember you.

I had been in a dark night of the soul for a number of years beginning

with a move from San Diego to the Palm Springs area. My husband
and I had experienced leaving our friends, our church, and the house
we loved, changing our professions and starting a new life. Against this
backdrop of weariness and fatigue, I heard a distressed voice on the other
end of the phone line one morning when I tried to call my mother. The
voice was not my mother's but her neighbor's crying and telling me my
mother had fallen and was being rushed to the hospital by paramedics.
As I cared for my mother's neck fracture, I began a long journey to the
dark side of suffering. I empathized with her pain and the challenges of
therapy, rehabilitation, and a move for her to an assisted living center. I
struggled with feelings of desperation, depression, and loneliness.

During the year of my mother's trial, I drove four hours each way
between Phoenix and Palm Desert almost every week to coordinate my
mother's therapy, physician visits, and medications. Meanwhile, I juggled
a full-time job, numerous speaking engagements, my marriage, our
home, and a growing Quiet Time Ministries. We sold a home I loved,
bought another home, packed, and moved. And somewhere along the
way, I became numb from the stress and suffering, my heart broken
seemingly beyond repair.

During my mother's trial, I chose my word for that year: *trust.* I
knew I needed to trust God in a far deeper way, so I began studying all
the verses in the Bible on trust, one at a time, writing out the insights,
one after another, in my *Quiet Time Notebook.* I wrote messages on trust,
designed quiet times on trust, and spoke on trust at retreats and conferences. As a result, I found myself relying on the Lord for strength in
my trial. The Lord showed me that trust is **T**otal **R**eliance **U**nder **S**tress
and **T**rial.

In January of the new year, as I continued to trust in the Lord, I
decided to read through *The One Year Bible* as my Bible reading plan
for the year. I sat at a local restaurant having breakfast with the Lord
and opened my Bible to the reading for the day, Genesis 8. I read, "But
God remembered Noah." Sometimes God will make His Word leap off
the page, grab you by the throat, and throw you to the ground. (R.C.
Sproul's description of the illumination of the Holy Spirit.) The words
come alive in such a way that you see them and understand them as
you have never seen them before. That is exactly what happened to me

when I read those words. My eyes became riveted to the page. The Lord had my attention.

The next two hours of study became a sacred, holy experience. Truths leaped off the page so fast that I could not write them down fast enough. These truths gave me great hope, and they can give you great hope as well.

I saw that God remembered Noah. In your trial, you can know that God pays special attention to you, and He is going to lavish His love and care on you in a very specific and direct way. In Noah's case, at the outset, God sent a wind (Genesis 8:1 NLT). God will send something that will begin to lift the pressure and adversity. Keep your eyes open for the "wind" that will relieve the burden of your trial.

And then "the underground water sources ceased their gushing" (Genesis 8:2 NLT). In this world, unseen forces are continually at work against us. And we do know, according to Ephesians 6:12 (NLT), that we wrestle against "the rulers and authorities of the unseen world, against those mighty powers of darkness who rule this world, and against evil spirits in the heavenly places." We live in an arena of spiritual warfare, and the enemy will tempt those who love Christ to fall into despair and unbelief, to lose hope and doubt God's Word. But "greater is He who is in you than he who is in the world" (1 John 4:4). For Noah, those underground water sources ceased their gushing. In the same way, in your trial, the Lord can, in His time, cause that which is working against you to cease.

Genesis 8:2 (NLT) tells us that "the torrential rains stopped." I saw that when God remembers us, He influences and changes outward trials and adversities as He rescues and relieves us in our circumstances.

In Genesis 8:3 (NLT) we see that "the flood gradually began to recede." Notice the word "gradually." The flood in a life will become less, but it does not always happen suddenly or at once. Noah did not actually leave the boat until a year after the rain began.

Then "the boat came to rest on the mountains of Ararat" (Genesis 8:4 NLT). God eventually brings us to a place of rest from all the floods that have come our way. I remember the tremendous rest I experienced when I knew that my mother was out of immediate danger of dying from her broken neck. Of course, had the Lord taken her home, she would have been face-to-face with Him in glory, and that is an even greater place of rest. But for my part, I did not want to lose my precious mother.

"Other mountain peaks began to appear" (Genesis 8:5 NLT). Now come the glimmers of hope of something new on the horizon. Only God can cause those mountain peaks to appear. The glimmers of hope often come from the promises of God in His Word. Think about the amazing glimmer of hope the Lord gave Corrie and Betsie ten Boom when He helped them smuggle the Bible into Ravensbruck concentration camp.

As I continued reading in Genesis 8, I saw that "Noah opened the window" (8:6 NLT), "sent out a dove" (8:8), and "lifted back the cover to look" (8:13). Noah finally became courageous enough to venture out and see what God was accomplishing. Sometimes we are so shell-shocked from the trial that we are almost afraid to look out the window of our trial and search out the plans and purposes of God. Sending out the dove was Noah's step of faith, indicating that he did believe God was causing the flood waters to abate. I realized as I read these phrases that I needed to step up my own level of maturity in the area of bravery and courage, believe God's promises in my own life, and eagerly look for Him to work in a powerful way.

Then I read God's words to Noah: "Leave the boat, all of you" (Genesis 8:16 NLT). Noah needed to hear from God before he would leave his refuge in the midst of the flood. And yet leaving the boat was absolutely necessary to continue running his race and experience the new life God had planned for him. I saw that I needed to embrace each experience, each change, in order to run in the direction of God's plans and purposes for my own life.

Noah responded to the Lord and "built an altar to the LORD" (Genesis 8:20 NLT). Noah rightly worshipped God, who is due all the reverence we can give Him. I saw that I needed to worship the Lord in the flood of trouble that had come my way.

The Lord was "pleased with the sacrifice" (Genesis 8:21 NLT). What a joy to know you have the smile of God. Nothing compares with experiencing the pleasure of God. Eric Liddell, the Olympic runner whose story was made famous in *Chariots of Fire,* often said, "When I run, I feel His pleasure." Oh, that we may run our race well and sense His pleasure even in the midst of trial.

Finally, "God blessed Noah and his sons" (Genesis 9:1). Blessing always follows brokenness and trials. I saw that as God's blessing had followed the flood in Noah's life, so the Lord would bless me following my own trials and adversities.

Once I finished my study of Genesis 8, I was moved to choose my new word for the year. I can truthfully tell you that I did not sit down at that breakfast with the Lord looking for or expecting such a powerful moment with God. But God had planned it. The Lord used Noah's example to give me hope. The Lord had chosen my new word for the year: *hope*. I was almost surprised as it came to my mind because I'm generally a very positive person, and I thought of myself as full of hope. But the Lord helped me realize through this time with Noah that somehow, deep within, I had embraced feelings of despair and was losing my hope. The Lord knows us better than we know ourselves. He sees all the way to the very depths of our hearts. He knew me better than I knew myself. And so began my new journey of learning all about hope.

My Response

DATE:

KEY VERSE: "But God remembered Noah" (Genesis 8:1).

FOR FURTHER THOUGHT: Where are you in your journey of hope? What has been going on in your life, and what is God teaching you? In what way do you need hope today?

MY RESPONSE:

Day Three

THEREFORE
I HAVE HOPE

*This I recall to my mind, therefore I have hope. The L*ORD*'s lovingkindnesses indeed never cease, for His compassions never fail. They are new every morning; great is Your faithfulness. "The L*ORD *is my portion," says my soul, therefore I have hope in Him.*

LAMENTATIONS 3:21-24

The promises of God give our hope wings to soar above our trials and circumstances on earth. In his own desperate hours, Jeremiah discovered the relationship between hope and the promises of God. "This I recall to my mind, therefore I have hope. The LORD's lovingkindnesses indeed never cease, for His compassions never fail. They are new every morning; great is Your faithfulness."

After I chose *hope* as my word for the year, I began learning what hope is from God's point of view in His Word. One day I was reading through Jeremiah's experience of suffering in Lamentations 3. Jeremiah's words described exactly how I felt:

I am the man [woman] who has seen affliction...he has driven and brought me into darkness without any light; surely against me he turns his hand again and again the whole day long...he has besieged and enveloped me with bitterness and tribulation; he has made me dwell in darkness like the dead of long ago. He has walled me about so that I cannot escape; he has made my chains heavy; though I call and cry for help, he shuts out my prayer; he has blocked my ways with blocks of stones; he has made my paths crooked... he has filled me with bitterness...my soul is bereft of peace; I have forgotten what happiness is; so I say, "My endurance has perished; so has my hope from the LORD" (Lamentations 3:1-18 ESV).

As I read these words, I said in my heart, *Yes, yes, yes...I am familiar with these feelings.* I was experiencing the dark side of suffering. I did feel a heaviness on me, walled in by suffering, with no end in sight. Through Jeremiah, God was revealing to me the deep pain in my heart. Over the years, I had learned to walk and live by faith in what God says in His Word. Yet the feelings of pain were there along with the adverse circumstances I had endured. I thought about all the pain Jeremiah had endured, reflecting on what I had learned about him in seminary. I had read many commentaries on Jeremiah, and I had often thought about how Jeremiah was God's object lesson to the people of Israel. He suffered much. God asked him not to marry but instead to be His voice to the people in their rebellion and to go with them into captivity to Babylon. No wonder Jeremiah has been called "the weeping prophet."

I continued reading Jeremiah's words in Lamentations 3:20: "My soul continually remembers it and is bowed down within me." I thought, *Well, my soul is certainly bowed down within me as well.* Then I read the next verse, "But this I call to mind, and therefore I have hope." My eyes lit up. Hope. That was my word that year. *Hope.* Jeremiah somehow found hope because of something he called to mind. What was it? The next verses gave the answer. I imagined Jeremiah thinking about these truths and finding hope.

The steadfast love of the LORD never ceases; his mercies never come to an end; they are new every morning; great is your faithfulness. "The LORD is my portion," says my soul, "therefore I will hope in him." The LORD is good to those who wait for him, to the soul who seeks him. It is good that one should wait quietly for the salvation of the LORD (Lamentations 3:22-26 ESV).

As I thought about what Jeremiah was calling to mind, the Lord revealed a very powerful principle to me. The promises of God have great power and give you hope. All that Jeremiah called to mind were promises from God. His steadfast love never ceases. His mercies never come to an end. They are new every morning. His faithfulness is great. He is our portion. He is good to those who wait for Him and seek Him. In those quiet moments, the Lord saw all the way to my heart, as only He can see, and He gave me a prescription for hope: the promises of God.

Jeremiah felt as if his prayers were being shut out, yet his soul knew something different. His soul said, "The LORD is my portion...therefore I will hope in him." When we pay attention to the things of the soul, we will turn to the promises of God in His Word. And that is what Jeremiah knew he needed to do in his darkness. He reminded himself of God's character and His Word, and he recognized two unstoppable forces at work in his life though everything seemed to be against him. God's love and mercy will conquer all adversity and are new every morning. Those realities provide the promise of a new day regardless of what we are facing.

I thought about the way the promises of God in His Word have impacted my life throughout my journey with the Lord. I have been in such deep, dark holes that I was certain I would never find a way out. I have thought even the Lord could not find me there. But in those times, God surprises me with something in the Bible that is significant to my particular circumstance. It might be something related to who God is, what He does, or what He says. What I have seen in His Word has given me a new point of view, a new perspective that has turned the tide and changed the face of my trial. God has comforted and calmed my heart. The promises of God have given me relief from an unexpected direction.

After the Lord showed me the power of His promises in Jeremiah's life, I began immersing my heart, my mind, my soul in His promises.

According to the psalmist, the promises of God revive our hearts (Psalm 119:50). Peter tells us that the promises of God enable us to experience God Himself (2 Peter 1:4). So here is what I have come to understand. As we immerse and bathe ourselves in what God promises in His Word, we come face-to-face and heart-to-heart with God Himself. When that happens, God is the voice of comfort in our lives. And then He Himself is the One who is our comfort. In the deepest trials of life, we often have no earthly options, and we are left to ourselves and to God. If God does not comfort, we will not be comforted. But when He comforts, we are comforted indeed. No word on earth can compare with God's Word. No voice on earth can compare with His voice. When He comes alongside you in your suffering and ministers to your hurting heart, you will experience a healing that is incomparable to any other on earth.

And in the experience of His comfort and care, you will know a new and deeper intimacy with the One who loves you more than life, your Lord and Savior, Jesus Christ. Through it all, you will travel to a new place in your relationship with the Lord. In his little book *The School of Calvary,* John Henry Jowett says this:

> If by the enlargement of my life I let in human sorrow, I also let in divine consolation. A big, holy purpose makes me more sensitive toward the sin and hostility of man, but it also makes me more sensitive toward God. If the sufferings abound, "so our comfort aboundeth also." If I said nothing more than this, this alone would suffice: if we suffer with Christ, Christ Himself becomes a great reality. When life is a picnic we play with theology: when life becomes a campaign we grope for a religion. It is one thing sounding when your boat is in the open sea: it is another thing sounding when the menacing rocks are on every side. When we suffer with Christ we come to know Christ, to come face to face with reality, and the idle superfluities drop away.[1]

There is a view of Christ and a view of His promises that only comes to light in the crucible of suffering. Christ comes to our aid and comfort according to our need. Only He can lift you out of your place of despair.

And would Jesus not be the One who can meet my deepest need? He is the One who is the "man of sorrows" and "well-acquainted with suffering" (Isaiah 53). If He knows suffering well, then He knows exactly how to walk with me in my pain and apply His balm to my wounds. The soothing ointment flows as He speaks His promises to my heart and soul and mind and spirit. *Catherine, you can do all things through Christ who strengthens you* (Philippians 4:13). *Catherine, I will supply all your needs* (Philippians 4:19). *Catherine, after you have suffered a little while, I Myself will perfect, confirm, strengthen, and establish you* (1 Peter 5:10). *Catherine, do not fear, I am with you. Do not anxiously look around. Surely I will help you* (Isaiah 41:10). Such are the promises of God from the Word of God spoken to the heart of man. They are personal. They are powerful.

My Response

DATE:

KEY VERSE: "This I recall to mind, therefore I have hope. The LORD's lovingkindnesses indeed never cease, for His compassions never fail. They are new every morning; great is Your faithfulness. *'The LORD is my portion,'* says my soul, *'therefore I have hope in Him'*" (Lamentations 3:21-24).

FOR FURTHER THOUGHT: Have you made the discovery of Jeremiah—that hope is available in the promises of God? What was a new thought or application to you today? Close your time with the Lord today by adding your name to these promises personalized from God's Word, and then thank the Lord for the hope they give: _____ _____, you can do all things through Christ who strengthens you (Philippians 4:13). _____, I will supply all your needs (Philippians 4:19). _____, after you have suffered a little while, I Myself will perfect, confirm, strengthen, and establish you (1 Peter 5:10). _____, do not fear, I am with you. Do not anxiously look around. Surely I will help you (Isaiah 41:10).

MY RESPONSE:

Day Four

THE UNIVERSITY
OF SUFFERING

*These things I have spoken to you, so
that in Me you may have peace. In the
world you have tribulation, but take
courage; I have overcome the world.*

JOHN 16:33

Every child of God attends the university of suffering; Jesus Himself promises our enrollment in this school. Jesus said, "These things I have spoken to you, so that in Me you may have peace. In the world you have tribulation, but take courage; I have overcome the world" (John 16:33). The Greek word translated "tribulation" is *thlipsis* and implies oppressive affliction and distress. Suffering is the opportunity to test the promises of God.

Virtually everyone comes to a point where he or she asks, "Why do pain and suffering exist?" Suffering and death came into the world as a result of evil and sin. When Adam and Eve chose to sin and go their own way in the garden of Eden, independent of God, their actions affected all of mankind: Death entered the world (1 Corinthians 15:22) and pain and suffering became a part of life (Genesis 3:16-19). D.A. Carson, research professor of New Testament at Trinity Evangelical Divinity School, speaks to the source of suffering:

> Between the beginning and the end of the Bible there is evil and there is suffering. But the point to be observed is that from the perspective of the Bible's large-scale story line, the two are profoundly related: evil is the primal cause of suffering, rebellion is the root of pain, sin is the source of death.[1]

Our understanding of the mystery of suffering is limited. Some questions in our minds will never be answered until we are face-to-face with God in eternity. And yet God has revealed certain knowable truths: "The secret things belong to the LORD our God, but the things revealed belong to us and to our sons forever, that we may observe all the words of this law" (Deuteronomy 29:29). We know that one day we will see a complete end to sin, evil, pain, suffering, and death (Revelation 21:1-4). And in the midst of our suffering now, Jesus has promised a way through our trials. And that way is wrapped in His promise of John 16:33: We can have peace, and Jesus has overcome the world.

As a young girl, I first learned about what I considered the grim reality of suffering through reading the biography of Darlene Diebler Rose, titled *Evidence Not Seen*. When I began reading the book, I had no idea who she was and had never even heard her name, but I soon became mesmerized by her story. Darlene and her husband, Russell, became missionaries in New Guinea, but were soon faced with the terrors of World War II. One day, enemy troops arrived at their missionary house and announced they were taking the men away. Darlene ran through the house, gathering provisions for her husband, who was nowhere to be found. She looked out of the window and to her horror saw her husband already in the back of the truck. Her breath escaping her, she ran toward her husband of only five years, handed him her pillowcase of items, and looked deeply into the face that had become so dear to her. He leaned down and said gently to her, "Remember one thing, dear, the Lord will never leave you or forsake you." And then the truck pulled away. Those were the last words she ever heard from her husband, for she never saw him again.

I remember putting down the book after I read her husband's words, and I sobbed and sobbed and sobbed. Somehow, as a young girl, I had been drawn into this woman's situation, and I felt as though I was walking alongside her in the harsh reality of her suffering, which eventually included her own imprisonment. C.S. Lewis has called suffering the problem of pain. In my young life, I had experienced the usual difficulties of childhood. But Darlene Rose endured what I considered to be the "no hope" kind of suffering. Unless God intervenes and does something in these situations, we have no hope. Perhaps even now you do not see any way out, and you do not think you can make it. And yet Darlene Rose was able to rest in the promises of God and sing hymns in her prison cell. Reading about the life of Darlene Rose was the beginning of my journey of learning in this university of suffering. I am still a learner.

In the university of suffering, assuming the posture of a student, a learner, yields a rich reward of hope. You are not alone in this school. Paul said, "I have *learned* to be content in whatever circumstances I am…in any and every circumstance, I have *learned* the secret of being filled and going hungry, of having abundance and suffering need" (Philippians 4:11-12). "[Jesus] *learned* obedience from the things He suffered" (Hebrews 5:8). The writer of Hebrews said, "All discipline for the moment seems not to be joyful, but sorrowful, yet for those who have been *trained* by it, afterwards it yields the peaceful fruit of righteousness" (Hebrews 12:11).

In the university of suffering, our powerful teacher is the Lord Himself. He has the supernatural ability to use our suffering for good, to create something new, and to transform us into masterpieces of great beauty, bringing honor and glory to Him. Peter promises this transformation in his first letter: "After you have suffered for a little while, the God of all grace, who called you to His eternal glory in Christ, will Himself perfect, confirm, strengthen and establish you" (1 Peter 5:10).

In Hannah Hurnard's allegory *Hinds' Feet on High Places,* the Chief Shepherd calls the creature Much Afraid to leave the Valley of Humiliation and journey with Him to the High Places and the Kingdom of Love. On this journey He makes Much Afraid into a new creature and gives her two unusual companions, Sorrow and Suffering. Much Afraid faces a time of testing and training as she journeys across treacherous terrain through valleys and adversities. Sorrow and Suffering are faithful to take Much Afraid to the High Places, her greatly desired destination. And when she arrives there she receives a new name—Grace and Glory. Her companions are transformed into Joy and Peace. Sorrow and Suffering have not caused her devastation and destruction but transformation.

John Newton's words in the hymn "I Asked the Lord That I Might Grow" describe the transformation process in this university of suffering:

> These inward trials I employ
> From self and pride to set thee free;
> And break thy schemes of earthly joy,
> That thou mayest seek thy all in Me.

The university of suffering teaches you the value of suffering and sifts your priorities and affections. The Lord desires an intimate relationship with each child of God, and He knows whether we are close to Him or we have set Him aside and walked away. A person can be very busy in the church and yet be far away from the Lord. The university of suffering sifts your priorities and affections because it puts you in a position of need so great that only the Lord can fill that need. You learn in an instant that everything else is unimportant compared to Him. If something else is captivating your attention, suffering helps you let it go so you can grab on to Him. Suffering reveals your earthly attachments, anything that is more valuable to you than the Lord. You must hold everything in your life with an open hand, knowing it all belongs to God. Suffering is always an invitation to go deeper in your relationship with the Lord, knowing He is your great treasure.

The university of suffering makes you a mighty warrior in the spiritual realm. It makes you a radical disciple for the kingdom of God. How? Suffering produces godliness, faithfulness, obedience, strength, and endurance in your life. Paul says, "We also exult in our tribulations, knowing that tribulation brings about perseverance; and perseverance, proven character; and proven character, hope; and hope does not disappoint, because the love of God has been poured out within our hearts through the Holy Spirit who was given to us" (Romans 5:3-6). I see a weak church in this day as I watch people giving up so easily in their pilgrimage with the Lord. We must be strong. Jesus invites you to follow Him and be a radical disciple for the kingdom: "Follow Me and I will make you fishers of men" (Matthew 4:19). Suffering makes a person strong and powerful—a mighty warrior in the army of Christ.

The university of suffering teaches you confession and repentance. Suffering humbles you. Peter encourages you to "humble yourselves under the mighty hand of God, that He may exalt you at the proper time" (1 Peter 5:6). This humbling action of suffering leads you to fall before the Lord in confession and repentance. Always remember that God never despises a broken and contrite heart (Psalm 51:17). John says, "If we confess our sins, He is faithful and righteous to forgive us our sins and to cleanse us from all unrighteousness" (1 John 1:9). You are encouraged to "repent and return, so that your sins may be wiped away, in order that times of refreshing may come from the presence of the Lord" (Acts 3:19). Repentance is like discovering you have made a wrong turn on your journey and instead of continuing down that road, you turn around and take the right road. Suffering invites you to confess all known sin, turn from it, and walk closely with the Lord.

The university of suffering will develop endurance in your life. Many in the church today are ready to give up. The fire has gotten so hot that many seem to think the only answer is to escape, to run away. The Lord has a better way—instead of escape, you can endure. The writer of Hebrews encourages us to "lay aside every encumbrance and the sin which so easily entangles us, and let us run with endurance the race that is set before us" (Hebrews 12:1). The Greek word translated "endurance" is *hupomone* and means "the spirit which bears things not simply with resignation but with blazing hope. It is the spirit which bears things because it knows these things lead to a goal of glory."[2] Suffering produces the very endurance that will enable you to reach the finish line of the race set before you.

The university of suffering will change your focus from religion to an intimate relationship with the Lord. You will commune with Him and listen to what He says in His Word. Paul says, "For momentary, light affliction is producing for us an eternal weight of glory far beyond all comparison, while we look not at the things which are seen, but at the things which are not seen; for the things which are seen are temporal, but the things which are not seen are eternal" (2 Corinthians 4:17-18). Suffering turns your eyes to the unseen, eternal realities revealed in the Word of God.

The university of suffering will show you God's character. God has said, "Cease striving and know that I am God" (Psalm 46:10). Only through the lens of suffering will you have the opportunity to see God do something only He can do. When you trust Him and take Him at His Word, you are going to see Him in action and experience Him first-hand in your own life. No longer are you going to observe others walking with Him and experiencing Him and wonder what it is all about. You will know Him for yourself in your own life. Suffering invites you to know and trust God as you face unmanageable adversity and impossible situations.

The university of suffering takes you to the throne of grace. The writer of Hebrews says, "For we do not have a high priest who cannot sympathize with our weaknesses, but One who has been tempted in all things as we are, yet without sin. Therefore, let us draw near with confidence to the throne of grace, so that we may receive mercy and find grace to help in time of need" (Hebrews 4:15-16). Suffering forces you to run to the throne of grace. Only God can answer the deepest needs of your heart. Sometimes, nothing on earth can help you; only God can. Suffering is an invitation to prayer and supplication in your deepest need. The promise is that you will find grace—and enough of it to help you in your time of need. God Himself guarantees this.

How can you learn from this university of suffering and pass the tests along the way? By discovering God's point of view, His eternal perspective, in His promises contained throughout the Word of God. In John 16:33 the promise to you is that you can overcome because Jesus is the Overcomer. He says, "take courage; I have overcome the world." The Greek word translated "overcome" is *nikao* and means to be victorious, to conquer, to prevail, and to win the case. How can you gain the victory? John tells us that "this is the victory that overcomes the world—our faith" (1 John 5:4). As you live in God's Word and gain His eternal perspective, you will make choices based on what you see and know to be true rather than what you feel or what someone else tells you.

Imagine Corrie ten Boom's miraculous release from Ravensbruck—

supposedly a clerical error but actually God's design. Perhaps the sun was shining. The moment she walked out those doors—doors that only opened from the outside—that moment was her *big moment*. She had stood strong. She had stayed the course. Now the Lord had a new plan for her life. What she had learned in prison, she would now proclaim to the world. And if you ever heard her speak, you would say, "Oh, how she could preach the Word of God." And how did she learn to preach like that? By speaking the truth and a message of hope to people who were living in the deepest hell man can create—to people who were, for the most part, on their way to die. She had learned much in her university of suffering that God would use in His plans and purposes.

John Henry Jowett, in his book *The Silver Lining*, says, "If He purposes my perfection, then all my circumstances will be made to conspire to the accomplishment of His will...Sorrow can accomplish what comfort would always fail to do." Sometimes only the tempest can bring out the music. Those who learn in the university of suffering have lives that sing to the world. Jowett goes on to say, "Have we not known men whose lives have not given out any entrancing music in the day of a calm prosperity, but who, when the tempest drove against them, have astonished their fellows by the power and strength of their music?" R.C. Sproul says, "Hope is the ability to listen to the music of the future. Faith is the courage to dance to it in the present." The music of the future plays through the promises of God, and faith dances and sings along.

My Response

DATE:

KEY VERSE: "These things I have spoken to you, so that in Me you may have peace. In the world you have tribulation, but take courage; I have overcome the world" (John 16:33).

FOR FURTHER THOUGHT: How have you experienced the university of suffering? What has God been teaching you? What is God's eternal perspective of your own suffering? What have you learned that will help you on your own journey with the Lord?

MY RESPONSE:

Day Five

TOUCHING HEAVEN
WHEN TESTED BY FIRE

*Dear friends, don't be surprised at the fiery
trials you are going through, as if something
strange were happening to you. Instead, be
very glad—for these trials make you partners
with Christ in his suffering, so that you
will have the wonderful joy of seeing his
glory when it is revealed to all the world.*

1 PETER 4:12-13 NLT

Y ou can touch heaven when you are tested by fire. This is what happens when you discover the promises of God and learn how to use
them. Peter reveals this dual perspective of the fiery trial and an accompanying future promise of glory: "Dear friends, don't be surprised at the
fiery trials you are going through, as if something strange were happening to you. Instead, be very glad—for these trials make you partners with
Christ in his suffering, so that you will have the wonderful joy of seeing
his glory when it is revealed to all the world" (1 Peter 4:12-13 NLT).

Peter has been called "the apostle of hope" because of the words of
comfort in his first epistle to the Christians in the Asia Minor provinces
who were enduring undeserved suffering. His brief letter contains 35

references to the Old Testament. These were the written promises of God for Peter since the New Testament was not yet complete. Peter encouraged believers to stand strong in the face of great trials and continue to hope in light of their imperishable and undefiled inheritance reserved in heaven (1 Peter 1:4). Peter's first letter is filled with promise after promise empowering these suffering Christians to persevere in their fiery trial. In 1 Peter 4:12-13, Peter gives us great truths we need to know when we find ourselves in a difficulty.

Peter wants you to know you are God's beloved child even though you are in the midst of a trial. Peter says, "Dear friends" (NLT) or "Beloved" (NASB). Sometimes, in the trial, we feel like an outcast child. I remember a time, many years ago, when I felt as though I was losing everything. I even asked my friends to pray for me because I felt as though I had lost the smile of God. I was a sad soul for a while as I walked that particular road of suffering with the Lord. Now I smile because I know, according to God's Word, that we cannot lose His favor. Sometimes we think that surely our God who loves us would never allow us to endure such pain, but then we remember that God's plan for His Son included the cross.

Amy Carmichael grappled with this apparent dichotomy between the difficult events of our lives and the love of God. In the prime of her life and of a burgeoning ministry, she suffered a crippling accident and spent her last 20 years in bed. She describes her experience this way:

> You look back at a certain moment which changed everything…a lightning-flash cleaving straight across the road on which you walked. You shut your eyes instinctively; when you opened them the road looked different. And it was different. Nothing will ever be again as it was before that lightning-flash. This, and this, and this you will never do again. And the road will grow duller and darker with every mile you go.[1]

But then Amy goes on to describe the realization of what it means to be beloved of God:

> A Voice speaks within you: "Things will never be as they were before? That is true; for they will be better. You will

never do this and this again? That also is true; for I have other things for you to do. They are not what you would choose? But they are indeed the best that Love can choose for you. The road will grow duller and darker with every mile you go? The path is like a shining light; like the sun that you have watched on many a lovely morning coming out of his chambers and rejoicing as a strong man to run a race. Does the light on that shining race-course of the sky grow less and less? No. it shineth more and more. So shall the path of My beloved be, not darker, but brighter as it nears the perfect day. This is the heritage of the servants of the Lord. *This,* not that."[2]

This is what Peter is saying to you in your trial: To God—the One who has created all things and is all-powerful—to Almighty God, you are His beloved. Dwell on this amazing promise when you are in a trial. And your trial does not define the love of God. The cross tells the story of God's love for you. God loves you and proved it on the cross. He made the ultimate sacrifice in offering up His Son for your sins. That really says everything you ever need to know about His love. D.A. Carson, comparing Job's trials to our trials, says, "In the darkest night of the soul, Christians have something to hang onto that Job never knew. We know Christ crucified. Christians have learned that when there seems to be no other evidence of God's love, they cannot escape the cross."[3] Always look at the cross, and you will know that you are His beloved. The Greek word translated "beloved" is *agapetos,* from the word *agape.* It means that you are dear to God, the object of His special love and attention.

I often think of my mother. When she is on the phone with me, she says, "Catherine, if only you could see all the way into my heart and know how very special you are and how much I love you." And that is what God is saying when He calls you His beloved: "If only you could see all the way into My heart and know how very special you are and how much I love you." That is what it means to be the beloved of God.

Peter tells you that your trial usually comes as a surprise: "Do not be surprised…" You can never say that you know you are going to find yourself in a fiery trial next week. When a trial comes your way, it will usually be unexpected. So take Peter's words to heart, and know that the trials will come and that they may surprise you, but they won't surprise God.

Peter wants you to know that the trial can be a very fiery ordeal indeed. The Greek word translated "fiery trials" is *purosis* and refers to calamities that test the character. These are intense experiences that purify. Fire always burns what can be destroyed and leaves what is solid and indestructible. The heat of the furnace in your trial will burn away the impurities but will never destroy the indestructible in you—your heart and soul, your eternal relationship with the Lord. Gold is purified in the heat of the fire. Job is the one who said, "But He knows the way I take. When he has tried me, I shall come forth as gold" (Job 23:10). I often think of Shadrach, Meschach, and Abednego, who refused to worship the gods of Nebuchadnezzar and, as a result, were thrown into a hot, blazing furnace (Daniel 3:23). When the king looked into the furnace, he saw a fourth person—the Lord was with them. The fiery furnace revealed their true identity: "servants of the Most High God" (Daniel 3:26). Nebuchadnezzar told them to come out of the fire and said, "Blessed be the God of Shadrach, Meshach and Abed-nego, who has sent His angel and delivered His servants who put their trust in Him, violating the king's command, and yielded up their bodies so as not to serve or worship any God except their own God" (Daniel 3:28). Though the fire rages about you in your trial, you can know that the Lord Jesus Christ is with you in the fire. And He will never leave you or forsake you (Hebrews 13:5).

Peter wants you to know that your trial is not meaningless, but accomplishes God's purposes. "For these trials make you partners with Christ in his suffering, so that you will have the wonderful joy of seeing His glory when it is revealed to all the world" (1 Peter 4:13 NLT). The title of one of Elisabeth Elliot's books is *Suffering Is Not for Nothing*. Elisabeth Elliot is such a perfect example of someone whose suffering accomplished God's purposes. Jim Elliot, her husband, was martyred by the Auca Indians. And yet, in her grief, Elisabeth Elliot stood strong. Not only that, she traveled into the jungles of Ecuador and took the gospel to the very Auca Indians who killed her husband. As a result, the Auca Indians came to know about Christ, and many were saved.

Peter wants you to know that your trial, the testing of your faith, will result in praise and glory and honor to God. "In this you greatly rejoice, even though now for a little while, if necessary, you have been distressed by various trials, so that the proof of your faith, being more precious than gold which is perishable, even though tested by fire, may be found to result in praise and glory and honor at the revelation of Jesus Christ" (1 Peter 1:6-7). Your trial is a test of whether or not you will take God at His Word. In every trial, the fiery ordeal seems to ask this question: "Which is more true—your feelings and circumstances or God's Word?" Even the people of Israel experienced this testing of their faith. In Deuteronomy 8:2-3 we learn something very important:

> You shall remember all the way which the LORD your God has led you in the wilderness these forty years, that He might humble you, testing you, to know what was in your heart, whether you would keep His commandments or not. He humbled you and let you be hungry, and fed you with manna which you did not know, nor did your fathers know that He might make you understand that man does not live by bread alone, but man lives by everything that proceeds out of the mouth of the LORD.

Paul tells us that "with most of them God was not well-pleased; for they were laid low in the wilderness. Now these things happened as examples for us" (1 Corinthians 10:5-6). What is going to keep us from being "laid low" in the wilderness of a trial? Walking by faith in the promises of God. And the result of walking by faith is praise and honor and glory at the revelation of Christ. Oh, what a day that will be!

Peter wants you to know that in your trial, you may feel as if something strange is happening to you, but it is not strange to God. The Greek word translated "something strange" is *xenos* and denotes a stranger from another place, unknown, coming from another country, unheard of and causing surprise and wonder. Sometimes the fiery trial launches you into what feels like an alternate reality. You feel as though you are not yourself because of the shock and pain. Peter is assuring you that God knows what you are experiencing, He has heard it, and it is not a strange thing even though it feels strange to you.

This is the eternal perspective and the promise in your fiery trial.

What you need more than anything in your difficulty is to hear from God Himself. That is what will enable you to touch heaven when tested by fire. Then you will know God is walking with you and that He cares. You will be able to respond as Peter said: "Be very glad—for these trials make you partners with Christ in his suffering, so that you will have the wonderful joy of seeing his glory when it is revealed to all the world" (1 Peter 4:13 NLT).

You see, when you embrace a promise from God, when you see God's view and hear Him speak truth to your heart, you touch a bit of heaven, the very throne room of God, where He rules. The readers of Peter's first letter surely experienced this kind of hope as they read promise after promise purposely given and delivered by Peter, a disciple of Jesus who walked with Him firsthand during His three-year ministry on earth. In the days to come we are going to talk more about how to touch heaven through the promises of God. We will look at what a promise really means and how to find it, embrace it, trust it, and live it. The promises of God pave the way through every storm in life and ultimately allow you to touch heaven when tested by fire.

My Response

DATE:

KEY VERSE: "Dear friends, don't be surprised at the fiery trials you are going through, as if something strange were happening to you. Instead, be very glad—for these trials make you partners with Christ in his suffering, so that you will have the wonderful joy of seeing his glory when it is revealed to all the world" (1 Peter 4:12-13 NLT).

FOR FURTHER THOUGHT: What does it mean to touch heaven when tested by fire? How have you experienced this in your own life? What did you learn today that you can carry with you throughout the day?

MY RESPONSE:

Day Six

QUIET TIME
WEEK ONE:
IN HOPE
AGAINST HOPE

In hope against hope he believed.

ROMANS 4:18

Prepare Your Heart

This week you have been learning about hope. In Paul's letter to the Romans, he uses Abraham as an example of someone with hope. Sometimes God gives promises that require "hope against hope." Today you will think about what that means so you can "hope against hope" the next time you need to. Turn to God now and ask Him to quiet your heart and speak to you in His Word.

Read and Study God's Word

1. Today you are going to look briefly at the life of Abraham. God gave an incredible promise to Abraham. He took Abraham outside and

asked him to look up at the stars in the sky. Read Genesis 15:5 and write out God's promise to Abraham.

2. God promised Abraham that his descendants would be as numerous as the stars in the sky. This promise seemed impossible because Abraham and Sarah, his wife, had no children and were past the age of childbearing. Miraculously, Sarah conceived and bore a son, Isaac. Then God asked Abraham to sacrifice Isaac to Him. Now Abraham had to make a decision. Would he believe the promise, hope in God, and obey Him? Read the following passages of Scripture and write out what you learn about Abraham:

Hebrews 11:8-19

Romans 4:18-21

3. Romans 4:18 says, "In hope against hope" Abraham believed. What does this mean? Today's English Version translates that phrase, "hoped, even when there was no reason for hoping." In the context of Romans 4, "hope against hope" means that Abraham "continued to believe God even when all grounds for human hope were gone."[1] This kind of hope waits expectantly and confidently for what is desired from God. The basis of this hope is God's promise alone. C.E.B. Cranfield, in his commentary on Romans, makes this point:

> Abraham believed God at a time when it was no longer a human possibility for him to go on hoping—human hope's utmost limit had already been reached and passed, and, so far as hope as a human possibility was concerned, he had given up hoping...Abraham's believing...is a defiance of all human calculations: his hope (signified by *elpidi*) is contrary to all human expectation (signified by *elpida*)...the hope must be understood as God-given, as a hope which was

altogether independent of human possibilities and human calculations.[2]

Write in your own words what it will mean for you to "hope against hope" the way Abraham did.

Adore God in Prayer

Pray the following words to the Lord written by Peter Marshall:

I do need Thee, Lord. I need Thee now. I know that I can do without many of the things that once I thought were necessities, but without Thee I cannot live, and I dare not die.

I needed Thee when sorrow came, when shadows were thrown across the threshold of my life, and Thou didst not fail me then. I needed Thee when sickness laid a clammy hand upon my family, and I cried to Thee, and Thou didst hear. I needed Thee when perplexity brought me to a parting of the ways, and I knew not how to turn. Thou didst not fail me then, but in many ways, big and little, didst indicate the better way. And though the sun is shining around me today, I know that I need Thee even in the sunshine, and shall still need Thee tomorrow.

I give Thee my gratitude for that constant sense of need that keeps me close to Thy side. Help me to keep my hand in Thine and my ears open to the wisdom of Thy voice.

Speak to me, that I may hear Thee giving me courage for hard times and strength for difficult places; giving me determination for challenging tasks. I ask of Thee no easy way, but just Thy grace that is sufficient for every need, so that no matter how hard the way, how challenging the hour, how dark the sky, I may be enabled to overcome.

In Thy strength, who hast overcome the world, I make this prayer. Amen.[3]

YIELD YOURSELF TO GOD

Meditate on the words of this portion of a hymn written by Charles Wesley:

> In hope against all human hope,
> Self-desperate, I believe;
> Thy quickening word shall raise me up,
> Thou shalt Thy Spirit give.
> Faith, mighty faith, the promise sees,
> And looks to that alone;
> Laughs at impossibilities,
> And cries: It shall be done!

ENJOY HIS PRESENCE

What situation are you facing today that is beyond earthly possibilities and requires you to "hope against hope"? How will you move beyond the temporal possibilities and impossibilities to the eternal promises of God? Write a prayer to the Lord expressing all that is on your heart.

REST IN HIS LOVE

"With respect to the promise of God, he did not waver in unbelief but grew strong in faith, giving glory to God, and being fully assured that what He had promised, He was able also to perform" (Romans 4:20-21).

Notes — Week One

Week Two

A LIVING HOPE
IN THE PROMISES

Days 7–12

Day Seven

THE MAGNIFICENT
PROMISES OF GOD

And because of his glory and excellence,
he has given us great and precious promises.
These are the promises that enable you
to share his divine nature and escape
the world's corruption caused by human
desires. In view of all this, make every
effort to respond to God's promises.

2 PETER 1:4-5 NLT

G od's promises draw you to His heart and give you the freedom to hope. Peter, our apostle of hope, encourages us, "And because of his glory and excellence, he has given us great and precious promises. These are the promises that enable you to share his divine nature and escape the world's corruption caused by human desires. In view of all this, make every effort to respond to God's promises" (2 Peter 1:4-5 NLT). When Peter speaks of promises, what is he referring to? The Greek word translated "promises" is *epaggelma* and suggests the intent, assurance, and declaration of God Himself. We see the verb form, *epaggellomai,* in Hebrews 11:11—Sarah "considered Him faithful who had promised." This action verb translated "promised" implies that God is revealing an important truth about who He is (His character), what He does (His works), or what He says (His Word).

63

We find God's words about who He is and what He does in His Word, the Bible; in the Word of God, God speaks (what He says). "All Scripture is inspired by God and profitable for teaching, for reproof, for correction, for training in righteousness; so that the man of God may be adequate, equipped for every good work" (2 Timothy 3:16-17). The Greek word translated "inspired by God," *theopneustos,* means "God-breathed, ordained by God's authority, and produced by the enabling of His Spirit."[1] God's promises are God's word, so they are completely trust-worthy and provide a firm foundation. That is why Jesus said, "Therefore everyone who hears these words of Mine and acts on them, may be compared to a wise man who built his house on the rock. And the rain fell, and the floods came, and the winds blew and slammed against that house, and yet it did not fall, for it had been founded on the rock" (Matthew 7:24-25). Promises are our firm foundation for a life built on hope.

So then, what are the attributes of God's promises? His promises are "great," according to Peter. "Great" is our translation of the Greek word *megistos* and means large, spacious, wide, long, and strong. The promises of God are powerful enough to handle any trial, suffering, or circumstance you face in life. And Peter says they are "precious." The Greek word translated "precious" is *timios* and means prized, valuable, and costly. The promises that God has given you are worth more than any earthly possessions; the promises of God make you a spiritual multi-millionaire. Peter reveals that the promises enable you to share God's divine nature, to share God's heart. The inference from the Greek word translated "share," *koinonos,* is of a partner or companion. No trial in life can touch the experience of drawing close and knowing the heart of your God. And finally, according to Peter, the promises of God allow you to "escape the world's corruption caused by human desires." The Greek word translated "escape" is *apopheugo* and means to flee or be rid of. The promises from God enable you to move from the things of this world to the things of God. That is why the promises of God lead to the certainty and confident expectation of hope. The promises change your perspective from dwelling on earthly feelings and emotions to focusing on the untouchable, unchangeable truths of God. These truths can never be taken away from you. And that is why, as a Christian, you can never lose your hope. The Lord, in His time, always provides a way through the trial.

Corrie ten Boom often spoke of an escape *(apopheugo)* experience that occurred during 4:30 A.M. roll call at Ravensbruck concentration camp. During one particular roll call, a cruel prison guard forced everyone to stand for hours, increasing the depth of their pain and suffering. Suddenly a skylark began to sing in the sky, and all the prisoners looked up. But when Corrie saw the bird soaring in the vast sky, she immediately remembered Psalm 103:11, "For as high as the heavens are above the earth, so great is His lovingkindness toward those who fear Him." In that moment, Corrie realized that God's love is greater than the deepest hate of man. The Lord sent that skylark to Ravensbruck during roll call for three weeks, turning the eyes of those prisoners from earthly hate to the depths of God's love. The promise of Psalm 103:11 became Corrie's personal escape during the grueling trial of roll call, even as she continued in her dark night of the soul.

Charles Spurgeon likens a promise of God as a check that we write from the vast resources and wealth of the Bible's bank account. Each check is signed by God Himself; He is the One making the promise. A promise is only as good as the one who makes it. And God is the faithful promise-giver (1 Corinthians 1:9, see also Psalm 31:15), and He cannot lie (Hebrews 6:18). Corrie ten Boom frequently shared that she would remember that there was a promise with her name attached to it.

F.B. Meyer has said, "There is hardly any position more utterly beautiful, strong, or safe, than to put the finger upon some promise of the Divine word, and claim it. There need be no anguish, or struggle, or wrestling; we simply present the check and ask for cash, produce the promise, and claim its fulfillment; nor can there be any doubt as to the issue." In *Streams in the Desert,* Mrs. Charles Cowman said, "The Creator will not cheat His creature who depends upon His truth; and far more, the Heavenly Father will not break His word to His own child…Since the world was made, God has never broken a single promise made to one of His trusting children."[2] William Gurnall writes this in *The Christian in Complete Armour:*

> Oh, it is sad for a poor Christian to stand at the door of the
> promise, in the dark night of affliction, afraid to draw the

latch, whereas he should then come boldly for shelter as a child into his father's house…Every promise is built upon four pillars: God's justice and holiness, which will not suffer Him to deceive; His grace or goodness, which will not suffer Him to forget; His truth, which will not suffer Him to change, [and His power] which makes Him able to accomplish.

You can know these assurances about the promises of God:

The promises of God are fulfilled by God Himself (Genesis 28:15).

The promises of God will never fail you (Joshua 21:45; 23:14-15; 1 Kings 8:56).

The promises of God agree with what is in His heart (2 Samuel 7:21).

The promises of God are the true words of God (2 Samuel 7:28).

The promises of God are fulfilled by God's hand and given from His mouth (2 Chronicles 6:4).

The promises of God are fulfilled by God because He is righteous (Nehemiah 9:8).

The promises of God are holy (Psalm 105:42).

The promises of God require faith (Psalm 106:24).

The promises of God comfort in affliction and bring revival (Psalm 119:50).

The promises of God have stood the test (Psalm 119:140).

The promises of God are not always fulfilled at once (Jeremiah 33:14).

The promises of God sometimes require patient waiting on our part (Acts 1:4; Hebrews 6:15).

The promises of God are the object of our hope (Acts 26:6).

The promises of God are found in the holy Scriptures, the Word of God (Romans 1:2).

The promises of God require strength in faith (rather than wavering in unbelief), giving glory to God, and a full assurance that God is able to perform His promise (Romans 4:20).

The promises of God are confirmed by Christ (Romans 15:8).

The promises of God are guaranteed by Jesus Himself (2 Corinthians 1:20).

The promises of God have been given to us (2 Corinthians 7:1).

The promises of God belong to those who know Christ (Ephesians 2:12).

The promises of God are given by God, who never lies (Titus 1:2).

The promises of God make us heirs (Hebrews 6:17).

The promises of God include an eternal inheritance (Hebrews 9:15).

The promises of God give us an unwavering hope because of His faithfulness (Hebrews 10:23).

The promises of God are precious and great and bring us near the heart of God (2 Peter 1:4).

Peter says we should "make every effort to respond to God's promises" (2 Peter 1:5 NLT). How can we cash those checks, each attached to a promise, so that we may have hope? The Greek word translated "respond" is *epichoregeo* and implies that the response is a supplementation of your faith. "Make every effort" is a translation of the Greek word *spoude* and exhorts us to earnest care and diligence in our response. I encourage you to respond in the midst of trials, suffering, and impossible circumstances of your life. We must find the promise, embrace the promise, trust the promise, and then live the promise. In the days to come we will learn how to make the most of the promises of God in the heat of the fiery trial and draw on the account that God has given us in His Word. (I have included a summary of how to find hope in the promises of God in appendix 4).

When once His Word is past,
When He hath said, "I will" (Hebrews 13:5),
The thing shall come at last;
God keeps His promise still (2 Corinthians 1:5).

ANONYMOUS

My Response

DATE:

KEY VERSE: "And because of his glory and excellence, he has given us great and precious promises. These are the promises that enable you to share his divine nature and escape the world's corruption caused by human desires. In view of all this, make every effort to respond to God's promises" (2 Peter 1:4-5 NLT).

FOR FURTHER THOUGHT: What is the most important truth you learned today about the promises of God? In what way do you need the promise of God in your own life?

MY RESPONSE:

Day Eight

FIND THE PROMISE

*By His divine power, God has given us
everything we need for living a godly life. We
have received all of this by coming to know
him, the one who called us to himself by
means of his marvelous glory and excellence.*

2 PETER 1:3 NLT

Y ou are a spiritual multimillionaire. Why? According to Peter, "God
has given us *everything we need* for living a godly life" (2 Peter 1:3
NLT). Then Peter elevates this claim to the realm of the great and precious
promises of God. He asserts, "For by these He has granted to us His
precious and magnificent promises, so that by them you may become
partakers of the divine nature, having escaped the corruption that is in
the world by lust" (2 Peter 1:4). In other words, you have a spiritual bank
account that becomes yours when you come to God through salvation
in Jesus Christ. And that bank account is sufficient for your every need,
trial, and suffering. These words, "God has given us everything we need
for living a godly life," come from the humble but rough fisherman
Peter, who walked with Jesus, knew Him intimately, and saw Him in

action firsthand. Peter walked on water at Jesus' invitation, witnessed the Sermon on the Mount, confessed Jesus as Messiah, witnessed the transfiguration, sat with Him in Gethsemane, saw Him scourged and crucified, saw Him raised from the dead, and received forgiveness from Him for his denials. This same Peter was given everything he needed to lead the early church. Peter was able to say with confidence that you have everything you need in the promises of God.

John Henry Jowett, in his commentary on 1 Peter, gives this explanation:

> Now, what is a promise? In our modern usage it is rather a light-weight word. It is often used as synonymous with "wish," and it carries no heavy significance. But the word as used in the New Testament has a far wider and vaster content. A promise of the Lord has a threefold purpose: it reveals an ideal, it kindles an ambition, it inspires a hope. We may take any promise we please in the Word of God and we shall find it enshrines the secret of this threefold mystery.[1]

God's promises reveal an ideal, a profound truth requiring contemplation and study. This contemplation lifts us above the low place where we were in our thinking, kindling a holy ambition within us. Jowett says, "A gospel promise transforms ambition into a mighty hope, and in the strength of a great expectancy the promised thing becomes possessed. So it is with all the promises of the Lord. They are exceeding great, the ideal stretches across the life and fills the firmament; and they are precious, pregnant with the possibility of inconceivable enrichment."[2] The Lord takes our hope into His realm of the eternal perspective, to those things that are unseen yet nevertheless real and true. You are able to see what you never saw before. You realize such realities as these: "God, who began the good work within you, will continue his work until it is finally finished on the day when Christ Jesus returns" (Philippians 1:6 NLT) and "God causes everything to work together for the good of those who love God and are called according to his purpose for them" (Romans 8:28 NLT). And you possess them as your very own, **H**olding **O**n with **P**atient **E**xpectation, eagerly watching to see how God is going to fulfill His promise.

When you think of God's promises as a bank account, you may wonder, *Well, how rich am I?* And that's a very good question. In your earthly life, if you do not know how much money you have, you do not know what you can afford to buy. In fact, you may be unlikely to spend any money at all. Similarly, most people have no idea of their spiritual wealth. In fact, many have never even opened their Bibles and do not know what God says. If you do not know what is in the Word, you are unlikely to write any checks on God's promises. And if you do not write any checks, then biblical hope, that confident assurance and expectation, is an improbable pipe dream. You cannot stand on a promise you do not possess.

I once heard of a woman who was challenged to discover every promise in the Bible. She became what she called a "promise person," establishing her life firmly on the promises of God. What is it going to take for you to be a promise person and make withdrawals on your spiritual bank account? You must open the pages of your Bible and find out what it says. You need to *know* the Word of God. Those seasoned warriors of the Lord who are radical disciples for His kingdom are the ones who really know what He says in His Word. When you know the Word, you have lots of checks to write and spiritual money to spend.

I have listened to many audio messages by Corrie ten Boom. Her vast depth and knowledge of the Bible surprises me again and again. Her ability to recite verses and explain their meaning would challenge most pastors. Just listening to her speak inspires me to open my Bible and study what it says. No wonder she had hope when she was in Ravensbruck and possessed so much of the Word to give away to others. Make no mistake—life seemed impossible for Corrie as she wrestled and struggled to live by faith. But there, in the hell of that place, she was a spiritual multimillionaire who was spending much spiritual money and reaping much benefit for the kingdom of God. Her captors thought they possessed the greatest power on earth and were in complete control when, in fact, a little Dutch woman had at her right hand all the power of the universe at work on her behalf.

I was in Chicago for a speaking engagement and spent a day at the archives of D.L. Moody at Moody Bible Institute. While at the Moody Museum, I learned a unique and interesting fact about D.L. Moody—he kcpt his preaching notes organized according to topics and messages in numerous large blue linen envelopes. At the archives I examined first-hand many of his handwritten preaching notes. Touching his notes made me feel as though I was sitting there with Moody himself. I discovered a man who knew the Bible. He wrote out one exposition after another on a plethora of Bible passages. One message in particular caught my eye—it was on Abraham and the promises of God. Moody scribbled this thought about God's promises on one of the pages: "Not one false…Not one grown stale." How true and how profound that personal statement. Moody knew those promises so well and was able to say from his own experience that God's promises are true and never grow old.

What will help you to know the Word and find His promises?

First, determine to set aside a time and place and to spend quiet time each day alone with the Lord. If you would like to learn more about how to have a quiet time, I recommend that you go on the 30-day journey in *Six Secrets to a Powerful Quiet Time.*[3]

Second, choose a Bible reading plan that will help you know the Word of God as you read and study the Bible each day. You might use the reading plan in a devotional Bible or use an in-depth Bible study curriculum.

Third, choose some good devotional books that will help you learn the many precious and magnificent promises of God. One of the very best is *Daily Light,* compiled by Jonathan Bagster many years ago in London. This little volume has been a favorite of mine from the time I was a very young Christian. Each day is filled with Scripture from all parts of the Bible, organized according to a daily theme or topic. I am constantly amazed at how the Lord seemingly wrote each day's Scripture just for me. The Scripture readings contain promises every day that you can claim for your needs and circumstances. I like the edition that uses the New King James Version because it is easier to understand than the Authorized King James Version. I also enjoy the devotionals written by Mrs. Charles Cowman: *Streams in the Desert* and *Springs in the Valley.* Each daily reading includes Bible verses, inspirational quotes, and readings expanding on the meaning of Scripture. Other good sources of promises from God are *Morning and Evening* and *Beside Still Waters* by Charles Spurgeon—he is a champion expositor of the Bible and knew the Word better than just about anyone I have read or researched. *My Utmost for His Highest* by Oswald Chambers is an excellent devotional and includes promises from the Word along with brief inspirational commentary.

Some books specifically written about the promises of God will help you know how spiritually rich you are, including *God's Special Promises to Me* by Clift Richards with Lloyd Hildebrand, *God's Promises for Every Day* by A.L. Gill, *Praying God's Will for Your Life* by Lee Roberts, and *Faith's Checkbook* by Charles Spurgeon.

When you read the Bible or devotional books, you should always look for a verse that teaches you something about who God is, what He does, or what He says. That is, search for the verse on His character, His works, and His words for your life. When you find this verse, you have found your promise. Then, consider the context to understand what God is promising you. Your goal is to discover God's eternal perspective in the promise contained in His Word. You want to see all of life from God's point of view and let that change the way you live in the present. This eternal perspective will give you hope. That is what it means to live by the promises of God. But first, you must find the promise. And you can find the promise by opening your Bible and exploring its pages.

Here are some examples of promises from God—you will find more in appendix 2 of this book. Notice that I have included various translations of the Bible. Alternate translations will open up a promise, making it more meaningful to you.

> No good thing will He withhold from those who walk uprightly (Psalm 84:11 NKJV).
>
> Casting all your anxieties on him because he cares for you (1 Peter 5:7 ESV).
>
> I will turn their mourning to joy, will comfort them, and make them rejoice rather than sorrow (Jeremiah 31:13 NKJV).
>
> I go to prepare a place for you. If I go and prepare a place for you, I will come again and receive you to Myself, that where I am, there you may be also (John 14:2-3 NASB).
>
> Call to Me and I will answer you, and I will tell you great and mighty things, which you do not know (Jeremiah 33:3 NASB).

Come to me, all of you who are weary and carry heavy
burdens, and I will give you rest (Matthew 11:28 NLT).

Jesus said, "I am the way, and the truth, and the life; no
one comes to the Father but through Me" (John 14:6
NASB).

Finding the promise is one thing. Next you must embrace the promise, understand what the promise means, and then surrender to it. We will explore how to embrace the promise tomorrow in day 9.

Every promise in the Book is mine!
Every chapter, every verse, every line.
I am standing on His Word divine,
Every promise in the Book is mine!

CHILDREN'S CHORUS

DATE:

KEY VERSE: "By His divine power, God has given us everything we need for living a godly life. We have received all of this by coming to know him, the one who called us to himself by means of his marvelous glory and excellence" (2 Peter 1:3 NLT).

FOR FURTHER THOUGHT: Write out what it means to be a spiritual multimillionaire. How well do you know the Bible? What will it take for you to know the Bible more than you do right now? What is one idea that you would like to try that will help you know the promises of God better?

MY RESPONSE:

Day Nine

EMBRACE THE PROMISE

*But forget all that—it is nothing
compared to what I am going to do. For I
am about to do something new. See, I have
already begun! Do you not see it? I will
make a pathway through the wilderness. I
will create rivers in the dry wasteland.*

ISAIAH 43:18-19 NLT

Embracing the promises of God requires surrendering your heart, letting go of your ways, and saying yes to His ways. Isaiah 55:8-9 says, " 'My thoughts are nothing like your thoughts,' says the Lord, 'And my ways are far beyond anything you could imagine. For just as the heavens are higher than the earth, so my ways are higher than your ways and my thoughts higher than your thoughts.' " The truth that helps me surrender my own ideas and plans is Isaiah 43:18-19 (NLT): "For I am about to do something new. See, I have already begun! Do you not see it? I will make a pathway through the wilderness. I will create rivers in the dry wasteland." Yielding to God's ways becomes easier when you realize that the Lord is creating something new that you do not yet know or understand.

Embracing a promise is never a "name it and claim it" process where you determine the outcome of God's Word. Some people teach this kind of handling of the promises in God's Word, but this type of thinking is biblically incorrect. Claiming a promise of God never means telling God what He is going to do. Claiming a promise means to embrace it, trust it, and live it, laying your desires out before the Lord watching eagerly to see what God is going to do.

To embrace God's promise, you must study the promise and gain insight into its meaning. How can you study a promise of God?

- Look at the promise in more than one Bible translation or paraphrase.

- Study the meaning of the words using word study tools, such as the *Hebrew-Greek Key Word Study Bible, Wuest's Word Studies in the Greek New Testament,* and the *Theological Wordbook of the Old Testament.*

- Complete a topical study using *Nave's Topical Bible.*

- Complete a cross-reference study using *The Treasury of Scripture Knowledge* or a Bible with cross-references.

- Read about your promise in selected commentaries, such as The Expositor's Bible Commentary series, the *New Bible Commentary,* or *Matthew Henry's Commentary on the Whole Bible.*

- Study your promise using Bible study software. Although I use several, my favorite is Logos Bible Software. Software tools, especially Logos, allow for specific searches through a variety of Bible study reference books, giving you the opportunity to do in-depth reading on your selected promise and helping you to understand the context.

- Use the free downloadable Bible study tools at www.e-sword. net.

- Use the free online Bible study tools at www.crosswalk.com.

- For more information on devotional Bible study in your quiet time, I recommend you go on my 30-day journeys, *Six Secrets to a Powerful Quiet Time* and *Knowing and Loving the Bible.*

When you study a promise, pay special attention to its context. For example, when you read God's promises to Joshua in Joshua 1, you understand from the context that the Lord is commanding Joshua to go into the promised land. Obviously, this does not mean He wants you to travel to that area of the world. However, certain promises do teach biblical principles you can apply directly to your life, such as Joshua 1:8 (NLT): "Study this Book of Instruction continually. Meditate on it day and night so you will be sure to obey everything written in it. Only then will you prosper and succeed in all you do." This encourages you to study the Bible and yields powerful results in your life.

When you understand what God is saying and have arrived at the meaning of the promise, write out your thoughts in your journal or *Quiet Time Notebook*. Writing what you have learned will help you apply it to your own life. I like using the *Quiet Time Notebook* (available at www.quiettimenotebook.com) because its preprinted pages help me to organize what God has taught me.

Once you understand the meaning of a promise from God, yield to it with a heart of surrender. To yield means to give way to God's ways. This is not always as easy as it sounds. Your feelings and circumstances may lead you astray. For example, you read in Romans 8:28 (NLT) that "God causes everything to work together for the good of those who love God and are called according to his purpose for them." Perhaps you are feeling as though your life is impossible and nothing good will ever happen. Surrendering to God means you receive what He is saying and hold it in your heart, trusting that His Word is truer than your feelings.

Perhaps you are faced with a seemingly impossible task from God. The promise in Philippians 4:13 is that "I can do all things through Him who strengthens me." Now is your time for surrender to God. Instead of running away, you say, "Yes, Lord, I will press on because I can do all things as You strengthen me."

Perhaps you have yielded to sin. Sin has altered the course of your life, and you wonder if the plan of God still has room for you. Surrender, for you, means confessing your sin, reestablishing your fellowship with God, and allowing the Master Painter to complete the picture of your life. Does He still have a plan? Oh yes, He does! The promise for you is that you stand in grace and that God has prepared some works for you to do (Romans 5:2; Ephesians 2:10). God has a plan and a purpose for you.

Your sin may have been horrific, but when you look at the cross, you realize why the crucifixion of Jesus was such a horrible death—He paid the price for every sin you committed. "There is therefore now no condemnation to those who are in Christ Jesus" (Romans 8:1). You cannot continue in habitual sin if you desire to have the Lord do a great and mighty work in and through you. The Lord is holy and works through clean vessels. The Bible says, "If we confess our sins, He is faithful and righteous to forgive us our sins and to cleanse us from all unrighteousness" (1 John 1:9). Embrace this promise, yield to Him, and watch what He will do! The Bible says that He can restore to you the years the locusts have eaten (Joel 2:25) and that He can take a spoiled vessel of clay and make it into another vessel that pleases Him (Jeremiah 18:4). No sin is so great that He is not greater still. The painting of your life is not ruined beyond repair. Always remember that the Master Painter can do anything! Let go of your life of sin, grasp hold of the One who loves you, surrender and draw near to Him, and experience the great adventure of knowing God.

Perhaps you have experienced the death of a dream. And perhaps you are blaming the death of this dream on others in your life—or even God. You disagree with the way God has conducted your life. You have begun to dwell on the "if only's" of life. And maybe your heart has given in to bitterness. But then you are confronted with the promise of God in Romans 12:2: "Do not be conformed to this world, but be transformed by the renewing of your mind, so that you may prove what the will of God is, that which is good and acceptable and perfect." You must make a decision. Will you continue to be mired in your own thoughts, feelings, and earthly point of view, forever bitter, forever hating God? Or will you surrender to God's promise of a "good and acceptable and perfect" will for your life? Are you willing to believe that He is doing something new in your life (Isaiah 43:18-19)?

A friend of mine said to me, "So, Catherine, this is a decision of my will. Instead of assuming that God is the author of evil and destroying my life, I should stop hating God and assume that God's Word is true, that He is not the author of evil, and that He is accomplishing a 'good and acceptable and perfect' will for my life, right? You want me to change my mind?" I stared at him for a few moments and said, "Yes, that is exactly what I am saying." The bridge of surrender takes you across the river of doubt from your sinful pride to the eternal perspective of God Almighty.

Behind this submission to the promise of God is a much deeper surrender—one that yields to the mystery and nature of God Himself. Ken Gire, in *The North Face of God,* speaks to this mystery:

> The Lord is King, but for all the clouds, we can't see the far reaches of his rule. The foundations of his throne are righteousness and justice, but darkness obscures our understanding of how a sovereign God could tolerate all the wickedness and injustice that run rampant through the earth. We may never reach a summit of understanding where suddenly everything is clear. For some cliffs are unscalable; some crevasses unbridgeable. And we may find ourselves stranded beneath an overhang, unable to climb any higher. But even if we do reach the summit, only patches of the surrounding panorama may be visible because of the clouds.[1]

God is wholly other. He is uncreated and will always be incomprehensible and mysterious. We must bend the knee to God as our sovereign Lord.

D.A. Carson speaks of this mystery in his book *How Long, O Lord?* He says, "It is better to let the biblical texts speak in all their power. Many things can then be said about the God who has graciously disclosed himself, but all of them leave God untamed."[2] And is it not true that God's untamed wildness goes beyond His revealed splendor into the unseen nature of the triune God Himself? Would we be so arrogant to believe that God should be completely explainable and comprehensible to mere men? And yet He has stooped down to us and revealed Himself. We even have His revelation in written form—the Bible. Carson emphasizes the importance of pursuing what we can know about God and His ways by handling Scripture accurately:

After we have accepted that the "givens" are non-negotiable and done our best to see just where the mystery lies—at heart—it is bound up with the very nature of God—we must ensure that biblical truths function in our lives in much the same way that they function in Scripture. That way we will avoid implicitly denying one truth when we affirm another; we will grow in stability; above all, we will better know the God who has in his grace disclosed himself to rebels like us, taken up our guilt, participated in human suffering, and sovereignly ensured that we will not be tempted above what we are able to bear. In knowing him better we will learn to trust him; and in trusting him we will find rest.[3]

You will be helped in your surrender if you look at your circumstances through the eyes of God's promise instead of looking at God's promise through the eyes of your circumstances. Instead of saying, "God's promise says one thing…however, I am experiencing quite another," you can change how you handle that little conditional word, *however.* You can say, "I am experiencing one thing…however, God's promise says quite another." Learn to switch your use of *however,* and you will more easily embrace God's promise and yield to His ways.

Embracing God's promise with a heart of surrender is one of the greatest secrets to walking with the confident expectation and assurance of hope. I recently read a book written by Corrie ten Boom's long-time assistant, Pamela Rosewell Moore, titled *The Five Silent Years of Corrie ten Boom.* Many people do not realize that Corrie spent the last five years of her life in almost complete silence following a series of strokes. This active and vibrant woman was reduced to a life of very little movement and constant attention from caregivers. And yet she lived in that confinement with a spirit of unparalleled love and grace, noticeable by all who came to visit her.

Pamela Moore's book includes a little story that gave me an insight into Corrie's relationship with her Lord. Corrie had many desires and loved to make plans. But more importantly, she was totally yielded to God's ways in her life. God had called her to travel the world, sharing the message of His love and forgiveness. And she did just that for more than 30 years following her release from Ravensbruck. One day during a mission trip, Corrie arrived at the home of a friend and was taken to the guest room. She looked around and remarked how peaceful it was. She said, "I wish…" but did not finish the sentence. She looked up and said, "Father, You do all things well. Thank You." The friend who saw this exchange between Corrie and her Lord was profoundly impacted by what she witnessed. She realized that Corrie wanted to say "I wish I could stay here longer" but quickly turned from her natural desire to thank her heavenly Father for His plans for her ministry.[4]

One day, when Pamela complained about the difficult demands of their traveling life, Corrie responded, "Pam, live as rich as you are in Jesus Christ. He has plans, not problems for our lives…The life of a Christian is an education for higher service. No athlete complains when the training is hard. He thinks of the game, or the race." And then she quoted 2 Corinthians 4:17, "For momentary, light affliction is producing for us an eternal weight of glory far beyond all comparison."

Corrie always interpreted life according to the promises of God in His Word. She used to say, "It is not so much what happens, but how we take it, that is important." She lived out those words in a new way following the strokes that left her paralyzed and unable to speak. One young woman in her twenties remarked that when she brought flowers to Corrie, she saw such love in Corrie's eyes that she would never be able to get it out of her mind. A teenage boy who visited Corrie said that such a love came from her when he was in her room that he immediately stopped all the wrong things he was doing. Whenever someone entered her room, the expression on her face said, "This is exactly the person I have been waiting to see." The love of Jesus was shining through a completely willing vessel. Pamela, her assistant, noted such a tremendous change of lifestyle would have crushed the spirit of most people, but Corrie's attitude was absolutely unchanged—she was the same whether she was weak and silent or strong and active.

After reading this powerful story of Corrie's life, here is what I have concluded. I think the Lord knew He could do anything He pleased with Corrie because she made no demands of Him with her will. She delighted to say yes to Him and to His will. She was open and unencumbered and entertained no desires outside of the Lord's desires. And so He could speak through her as a prisoner in Ravensbruck concentration camp, as a tramp for Him all over the entire world, and as an invalid lying in a bed, paralyzed and unable to speak. May her tribe increase.

In the early years of D.L. Moody's ministry, he heard the British evangelist Henry Varley say, "The world has yet to see what God will do with and for and through and in and by the man who is fully and wholly consecrated to Him." Moody responded this way, "He said *a man*. He did not say a great man, nor a learned man, nor a rich man, nor a wise man, nor an eloquent man, nor a smart man, but simply *a man*. I am a man, and it lies with the man himself whether he will or will not make that entire and full consecration. I will try my uttermost to be that man."

Surrender to the promise, dear friend. Step out from the limitations of your own desires into God's vast eternal plan for your life. Let God have His way with you and then watch for that "something new" He is going to do. The issue is not how much you have of God, but how much God has of you.

My Response

DATE:

KEY VERSE: "But forget all that—it is nothing compared to what I am going to do. For I am about to do something new. See, I have already begun! Do you not see it? I will make a pathway through the wilderness. I will create rivers in the dry wasteland" (Isaiah 43:18-19 NLT).

FOR FURTHER THOUGHT: What does "embrace the promise" mean? Why is surrender so important if we are to embrace the promises of God? Where in your life do you need to surrender? Does God have all of you, and is He free to use you any way He pleases? Write a prayer to the Lord expressing all that is on your heart today.

MY RESPONSE:

Day Ten

TRUST THE PROMISE

For in hope we have been saved,
but hope that is seen is not hope; for who
hopes for what he already sees?
But if we hope for what we do not see,
with perseverance we wait eagerly for it.

ROMANS 8:24-25

When you trust the promise, you will see God's unseen, eternal perspective and possess a hope that waits eagerly to see what God will do in your life. Once you have found a promise and embraced it, you now need to *trust the promise*. Trust moves you from what God says to hope, that confident expectation in the fulfillment of God's promise. Trust means putting legs to what God has said in His Word, adding action to convictions. I like to think of trust as **T**otal **R**eliance **U**nder **S**tress and **T**rial. Trust sees the unseen realities contained in the promises of God in His Word and applies those truths to life's circumstances. Paul said, "We look not at the things which are seen, but at the things which are not seen; for the things which are seen are temporal, but the things which are not seen are eternal" (2 Corinthians 4:18). When trust applies those unseen eternal things, we have the kind of hope that can never be shaken, that perseveres, and that is steadfast and assured. Paul said, "For in hope we have been saved, but hope that is seen is not hope; for who hopes for what he already sees? But if we hope for what we do not see, with perseverance we wait eagerly for it" (Romans 8:24-25). The writer of Hebrews exhorts us to "hold tightly without wavering to the hope we affirm, for God can be trusted to keep his promise" (Hebrews 10:23 NLT).

Trusting God's promise means you actually write the check on the bank account of His Word containing all the promises of God. You fill in your name and hand the check to the Lord. This check is already signed by God Himself and guaranteed by His trustworthiness and faithfulness. Here's what Charles Spurgeon says:

> A promise from God may very instructively be compared to a check payable to order. It is given to the believer with the view of bestowing upon him with some good thing. It is not meant that he should read it over comfortably, and then have done with it. No, he is to treat the promise as a reality, as a man treats a check...He is by faith to accept it as his own...He must believingly present the promise to the Lord, as a man presents a check at the counter of the Bank. He must plead it by prayer, expecting to have it fulfilled. If he has come to Heaven's bank at the right date, he will receive the promised amount at once. If the date should happen to be further on, he must patiently wait till its arrival; but meanwhile he may count the promise as money, for the Bank is sure to pay when the due time arrives.[1]

What does it mean to write the check? It means that you attach your name to God's promise, apply it to your life, and turn it over to the Lord. Three disciplines will help you do this: memorize the promises, pray the promises, and personalize the promises.

MEMORIZE THE PROMISES

The more of the Bible you memorize, the more God's promises will be available to you to draw upon as cash reserves during the circumstances of life. "I have stored up your word in my heart, that I might not sin against you" (Psalm 119:11 ESV). Promises of God can be stored and hidden in your heart. Memorizing the promises of God will help you in the heat of the battle, for those hidden promises will come to your mind just at the right time when you need them.

PRAY THE PROMISES

"And we are confident that he hears us whenever we ask for anything that pleases him. And since we know he hears us when we make our requests, we also know that he will give us what we ask for" (1 John 5:14-15 NLT). Praying the promises of God produces an inner confidence and conviction. The Greek word for "confident" is *parrhesia* and refers to boldness and a joyful sense of freedom. The Greek word for "know" is *oida*—coming to the realization of something, in this case, the promises of God.

I love to pray the promises and often will personalize verses in the Bible and pray them back to God in conversation and communion with Him. The Lord says, "Call to Me and I will answer you, and I will tell you great and mighty things, which you do not know" (Jeremiah 33:3). This is the promise of what happens when we pray the promises of God. The Lord will answer us. He may not always give us the answer we expect, but you can count on the Lord to keep His promise to respond to your prayer. David said, "In the morning I will order my prayer to You and eagerly watch" (Psalm 5:3). Why eagerly watch? Because oh, how the Lord will answer your prayer.

I remember years ago when my friend Shirley Peters prayed that the Lord would use a little ministry I had just begun called Quiet Time Ministries to reach the world. I was astounded at the scope of her prayer. But she believed that God could do more than we could ask or imagine. You can imagine how excited I was early on when I received an e-mail from someone in South Africa who wanted to print multiple copies of my testimony and pass it out to students at universities throughout that country. Now I receive e-mails from people all over the world. We have a map at our Quiet Time Ministries Resource and Training Center, and we place a little pin on the map every time someone orders our resource materials from a new place. That map is filling up with pins from everywhere.

Sometimes when we pray the promises, the answers come exactly as we have asked but abundantly overflowing and multiplied.

Amy Carmichael, bedridden following an injury, shared that "on a certain evening there was a special prayer for the healing touch, and that night the pain was lulled and natural sleep was given. The blissfulness of the awakening next morning is still vivid and shining. I lay for a few minutes almost wondering if I were still on earth."[2]

I have a place on my *Quiet Time Notebook* prayer pages to record promises for each of my prayer requests. Sometimes I sit and leaf through the pages, reviewing how the Lord has answered my requests as I have brought His promises to Him with my name on them. I can truthfully say that He always answers—perhaps not in the way I would expect, but always in His time. I just marvel when I step back and see the greatness of His plan compared to my own little idea of how things would be or should be. He is the Master Painter, and I must be the willing canvas and allow Him to create the masterpiece He has in mind.

Personalize the Promises

Personalizing the promises of God lifts the Word of God from the pages of your Bible into your heart. Personalizing the promises is an art, a skill to be learned with time and experience. The best way to learn is to write out God's promises in your journal.

When you personalize the promises of God, you individualize the words as you read them or write them in your journal, making them personal to your life. For example, Paul gives the promise in Philippians 4:19 (ESV), "And my God will supply every need of yours according to his riches in glory in Christ Jesus." You can personalize this promise at least four ways:

- Place your name at the beginning of the verse, imagining the promise spoken directly to you. This is my favorite way to personalize a promise if I am sharing it with someone who needs encouragement from the Word of God. "Catherine, God will supply every need of yours according to His riches in glory in Christ Jesus."

- Substitute your name in place of the personal pronouns

contained in the promise. "God will supply every need of Catherine's according to His riches in glory in Christ Jesus."

- Personalize the verse to read as a promise from God, in the first person, to you. "I will supply every need of yours according to His riches in glory in Christ Jesus."

- Change the personal pronouns "you" to "me" and recite the promise to yourself as a reminder of what God is saying to you. This is my favorite way to personalize the promises when I am reading through Scripture or writing out verses in my journal. "God will supply every need of mine according to His riches in Christ Jesus."

Make a habit of writing checks on the promises of God as you personalize and apply the truth of Scripture. Become a "spiritual shopaholic" when reading God's Word, constantly attaching your name, personalizing what you see in the Bible. The enemy of your soul, the devil, may come just when you could be discouraged, and he will try to tell you you are poor, insignificant, and defeated. But you can rush to your spiritual bank account, the Word of God, and see how rich you really are—in fact, a spiritual multimillionaire. When you see your riches, go shopping on that account, and write lots of spiritual checks. An example might help you see what trusting the promise looks like in real circumstances. In figure 1, on page 93, you'll see a check with a promise from God that I am claiming. Notice that I have written the date and added my name in the "This promise is for" line. The verse, Philippians 4:13, is where a dollar sign would be on a check, and the actual verse, "I can do all things through Him who strengthens me," is written on the line below. The check is signed by the Lord Himself, the Creator of the universe, because the Word of God is written and guaranteed by God—"all Scripture is inspired by God" (2 Timothy 3:16). The memo line is used to write out the dates and occasions for each time you write the check on a promise.

Writing the checks and making withdrawals on your heavenly bank account results in a hope that waits eagerly for what God is going to do in your life circumstance. You will discover that the life of faith is, as Corrie ten Boom said, a **F**antastic **A**dventure **I**n **T**rusting **H**im.

Trust in the LORD with all your heart; do not depend on your own understanding. Seek his will in all you do, and he will show you which path to take (Proverbs 3:5-6 NLT).

Lord,
You made me a promise,
I know it is true.
And claim it by faith,
For it came from You.

Now,
I trust in the promise,
In hope I do stand.
Awaiting the day,
We'll walk hand in hand.

Then,
Faith at last will be sight,
Promises fulfilled.
I'll bathe in Your glory,
Rejoicing and stilled.

CONNI HUDSON

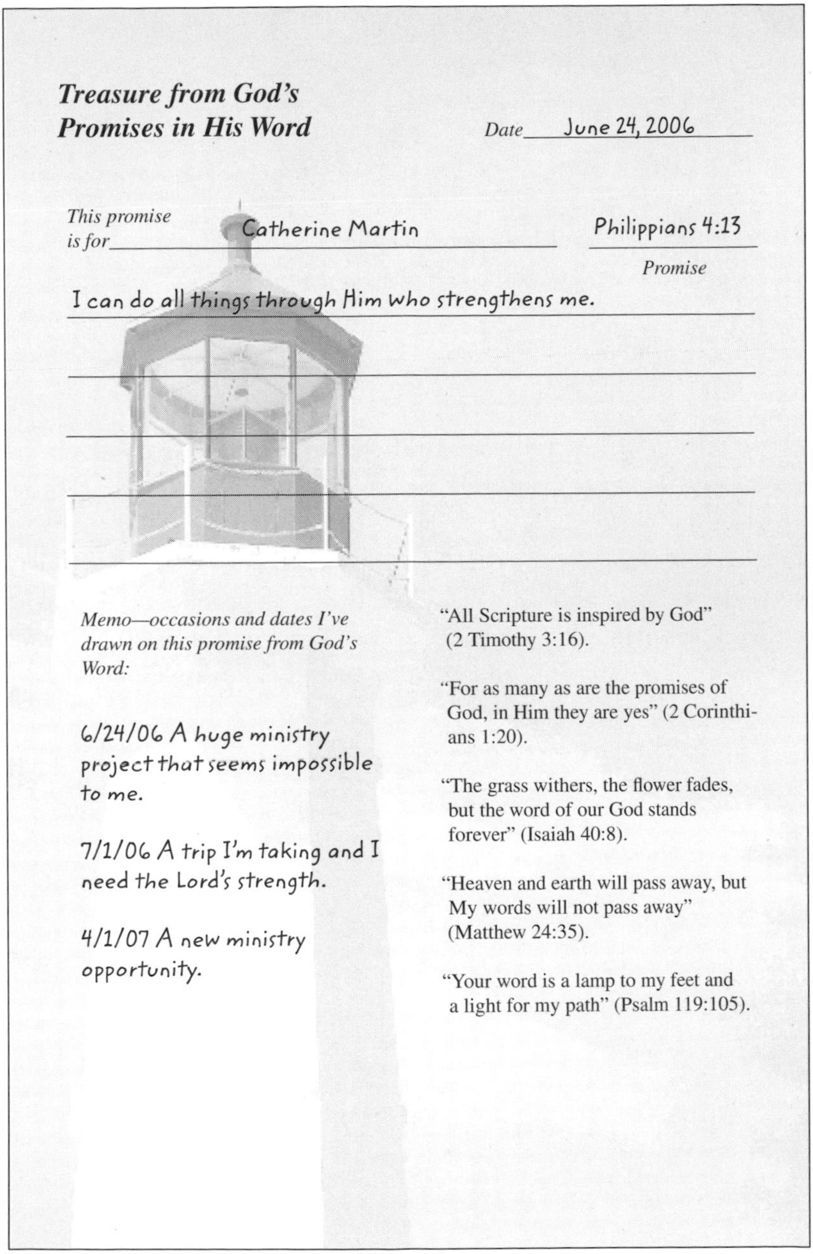

Treasure from God's
Promises in His Word

*Date*___ June 24, 2006 ___

This promise is for ___ Catherine Martin ___

Philippians 4:13
Promise

I can do all things through Him who strengthens me. ___

Memo—occasions and dates I've drawn on this promise from God's Word:

6/24/06 A huge ministry project that seems impossible to me.

7/1/06 A trip I'm taking and I need the Lord's strength.

4/1/07 A new ministry opportunity.

"All Scripture is inspired by God" (2 Timothy 3:16).

"For as many as are the promises of God, in Him they are yes" (2 Corinthians 1:20).

"The grass withers, the flower fades, but the word of our God stands forever" (Isaiah 40:8).

"Heaven and earth will pass away, but My words will not pass away" (Matthew 24:35).

"Your word is a lamp to my feet and a light for my path" (Psalm 119:105).

Fig. 1

My Response

DATE:

KEY VERSE: "For in hope we have been saved, but hope that is seen is not hope; for who hopes for what he already sees? But if we hope for what we do not see, with perseverance we wait eagerly for it" (Romans 8:24-25).

FOR FURTHER THOUGHT: How does writing the check on the promises of God help you trust the promise in your own life? In what area of your life do you need a promise from God today? Will you write the check on that promise? Find a promise that will help you today. Then turn to the end of appendix 2 and use the blank promise page to write out and personalize the promise. (These promise pages are available for the *Quiet Time Notebook* and are also part of the companion *Walking with the God Who Cares Journal*).

MY RESPONSE:

Day Eleven

LIVE THE PROMISE

*We also exult in our tribulations, knowing
that tribulation brings about perseverance;
and perseverance, proven character; and
proven character, hope; and hope does not
disappoint, because the love of God has
been poured out within our hearts through
the Holy Spirit who was given to us.*

ROMANS 5:3-5

Suffering leads to hope when, in the crucible of your trial, you live the promise. Living the promise means taking God at His Word and acting on His promises. What He says in the promise may or may not agree with how you feel or what you see in your circumstance. You live out Paul's statement: "We walk by faith, not by sight" (2 Corinthians 5:7).

The ultimate expression of living the promise is a "by faith" exultation (rejoicing in God) in the context of suffering. This rejoicing is only possible by the work of the Holy Spirit in your life and occurs gradually as you apply God's promises to your life. Paul said, "We also exult in our tribulations, knowing that tribulation brings about perseverance;

and perseverance, proven character; and proven character, hope; and hope does not disappoint, because the love of God has been poured out within our hearts through the Holy Spirit who was given to us" (Romans 5:3-5).

A natural progression occurs when you live the promise: Tribulation leads to perseverance (endurance). Endurance gives you an A on the test of character—your character is proven, and you are the genuine article, a child of God belonging to Christ. Proven character leads to hope, the kind of hope that does not disappoint. It will not let you down or make you ashamed. Biblical hope is the certain expectation in God and what He says. "Not one word of all the good things the Lord your God promised concerning you has failed" (Joshua 23:14). That hope leads to a firsthand experience of the love God poured out in your heart by the indwelling Holy Spirit. The experience of God's love is something no one can destroy because it is in the heart, protected by God Himself.

God's love is hope's reward. Its expression is your crowning glory. Corrie ten Boom learned this lesson following her release from Ravensbruck. She was speaking to a group about her concentration camp experience and the great love and forgiveness of God. After her message, a man made his way up to the front of the room where she was standing. Immediately, she remembered him as one of the guards at Ravensbruck who had been very cruel to her sister. She braced herself for the confrontation. The man walked up to her, the appearance of his face transformed, and said, "Isn't it great that I can be washed clean through the blood of Jesus!" Then he reached out his hand toward Corrie. But she could not bring herself to shake his hand, remembering the prisoners' terrible humiliation when they were paraded naked in front of the soldiers. And then she thought about Romans 5:3-5, how God promised to shed His love in her heart through the Holy Spirit. In an instant, she attached her name to that promise, wrote the check, and lived the promise. Corrie prayed that she could love this man as God loved him, and as soon as the prayer was given, she was able to reach out her hand. The Holy Spirit had done for Corrie what she could not do for herself, and the results were forgiveness, a love for her enemies, and a realization that God had used her for His purposes. You see, love is always hope's reward.

You always have a choice in your suffering. You can worry, you can borrow trouble, you can be anxious, you can panic, or you can remember that there is no panic in heaven and that God is never worried or anxious. You can find the promise, embrace the promise, trust the promise, and live the promise. Claiming the promises of God is never easy in the midst of a fiery trial, but it is possible. Oswald Chambers says that walking by faith is a fight always, not sometimes. That is why Paul encouraged Timothy to "fight the good fight of faith" (1 Timothy 6:12). Paul evaluated his own life by saying, "I have fought the good fight, I have finished the race, I have kept the faith" (2 Timothy 4:7). You can become accomplished in living the promises of God, as Corrie ten Boom was, in the power of the Holy Spirit and the presence of Jesus. Do not be surprised that when you begin to apply God's promises to your life and fight the good fight of faith, God will use you in a powerful way in the lives of others. Only heaven will tell the complete story of everything He has done in and through you.

Hannah Whitall Smith encourages you with these words:

> Let your faith, then, throw its arms around all God has told you, and in every dark hour remember that "though now for a season, if need be, ye are in heaviness through manifold temptations," it is only like going through a tunnel. The sun has not ceased shining because the traveler through the tunnel has ceased to see it; and the Sun of righteousness is still shining, although you in your dark tunnel do not see Him. Be patient and trustful, and wait. This time of darkness is only permitted "that the trial of your faith, being much more precious than of gold that perisheth, though it be tried with fire, might be found unto praise and honor and glory at the appearing of Jesus Christ."[1]

Amy Carmichael could have given up after her devastating accident that left her bedridden for the last 20 years of her life. After all, most people would believe her ministry was finished. She had founded and directed a powerful ministry in India at the Dohnavur Fellowship. But when people say "it's over," remember, that is man's opinion, not God's. In fact, Amy Carmichael was exactly where God wanted her—ready to do that something new (Isaiah 43:18-19) that God had planned and prepared beforehand (Ephesians 2:10). Amy found the promises. She embraced the promises. She trusted the promises. And she lived the promises. Instead of fading off into the sunset of despair, she did all she could do in this new place where she found herself. She began writing. And in those last 20 years of her life, she wrote the books that the world has come to know and love. You see, she had in mind something small in a little corner of the world, and God had in mind a much different, a much larger sphere of influence extending not only throughout the world but also through many generations. Only heaven will tell of the ripple effect of lives that learn to find the promise, embrace the promise, trust the promise, and live the promise.

O Thou beloved child of My desire,
Whether I lead thee through green valleys,
By still waters,
Or through fire,
Or lay thee down in silence under snow,
Through any weather, and whatever
Cloud may gather—
Wind may blow—
Wilt thou love Me? trust Me? praise Me?

No gallant bird, O dearest Lord, am I,
that anywhere, in any weather,
Rising singeth;
Low I lie.
And yet I cannot fear, for I shall soar,
Thy love shall wing me, blessed Saviour;
So I answer,
adore,
I love Thee, trust Thee, praise Thee.[2]

AMY CARMICHAEL

DATE:

KEY VERSE: "We also exult in our tribulations, knowing that tribulation brings about perseverance; and perseverance, proven character; and proven character, hope; and hope does not disappoint, because the love of God has been poured out within our hearts through the Holy Spirit who was given to us" (Romans 5:3-5).

FOR FURTHER THOUGHT: Have you learned to live the promise, acting on what you know to be true in God's Word? What is the most important truth you have learned this week in your time with the Lord that will help you to have hope?

MY RESPONSE:

Day Twelve

QUIET TIME WEEK TWO: HOPE THAT DOES NOT DISAPPOINT

Hope does not disappoint, because the love of God has been poured out in our hearts through the Holy Spirit who was given to us.

ROMANS 5:5

PREPARE YOUR HEART

In our theology of hope we must explore one of the most outrageous statements Paul ever makes: "Hope does not disappoint" (Romans 5:5). Why is this so outrageous? Because it seems as though in the course of life, our hopes are constantly dashed. When you read a statement in the Bible that seems so unbelievable and contrary to your life experience, you may conclude that it doesn't mean what you thought it meant. In fact, its real meaning will exceed your greatest expectations and take you to a new level in your walk with the Lord. That is why the child of God possesses such a marvelous resource in the Bible—it teaches, reproves, corrects; it trains you in righteousness, makes you adequate, and equips you for every good work (2 Timothy 3:16). What then can we learn about this hope that does not disappoint? That is the subject of our quiet time with the Lord today. Ask God to quiet your heart and speak to you from His Word today.

READ AND STUDY GOD'S WORD

1. Paul teaches a powerful principle in Romans 5:3-5. The process of a trial does not need to destroy hope and, in fact, can actually lead to hope. Read Romans 5:3-5 and write out what you learn about how the process of a trial can actually lead to hope.

2. A hope that doesn't disappoint is not the same as other kinds of hope you may have known in the past. Past hopes that bring disappointment cannot, in fact, really be considered in the same category as the hope that Paul is writing about here. The kind of hope that has been dashed over and over again may be a desire or wish, and these are not the same as biblical hope. If we hope in the biblical way, we will never be disappointed. That is what Paul is really saying here. This kind of hope is in God and the fulfilment of His promises. God Himself strengthens and confirms this kind of hope—it does not "put those to shame who cherish it by proving illusory."[1] We are never disappointed when we hope in this way because the end result is the experience of God's love in our hearts. This intimacy with God is knowing God at its highest and best.

Describe in your own words the difference between earthly wishing and desiring, and the hope described in Romans 5.

ADORE GOD IN PRAYER

Bring all your wishes and desires to the Lord. Then ask the Lord to fill your heart with His love by the power of the Holy Spirit. Personalize the words from this hymn by Edward Mote:

My hope is built on nothing less
Than Jesus' blood and righteousness.
I dare not trust the sweetest frame,
But wholly lean on Jesus' name.

When darkness veils His lovely face,
I rest on His unchanging grace.
In every high and stormy gale,
My anchor holds within the veil.

His oath, His covenant, His blood,
Support me in the whelming flood.
When all around my soul gives way,
He then is all my hope and stay.

When He shall come with trumpet sound,
O may I then in Him be found.
Dressed in His righteousness alone,
Faultless to stand before the throne.

On Christ, the solid rock, I stand;
All other ground is sinking sand,
All other ground is sinking sand.

YIELD YOURSELF TO GOD

Think about the following words by Kenneth Wuest:

Paul did not exult because of the tribulations themselves but because of their beneficial effect upon his Christian life. This the saint must learn to do. He must look at these trials and difficulties as assets that develop his Christian character. Paul says that they work patience…Remain under trials in a God-honoring way so as to learn the lesson they are sent to teach, rather than attempt to get out from under them in an effort to be relieved of their pressure…Denney, speaking of "patience" *(hupomoné),* says, it "produces approvedness—its result is a spiritual state which has shown itself proof under trial." This approved character produces and increases hope. Denney comments, "'The experience of what God can do, or rather of what He does, for the justified amid the tribulations of this life, animates into new vigor the hope with which the life of faith begins."[2]

ENJOY HIS PRESENCE

How do you need the biblical kind of hope, and how is God developing it in your life? What trials have come your way that are leading you through the Romans 5:3-5 process to hope? Write a prayer to the Lord expressing all that is on your heart.

REST IN HIS LOVE

"We can rejoice, too, when we run into problems and trials, for we know that they help us develop endurance. And endurance develops strength of character, and character strengthens our confident hope of salvation. And this hope will not lead to disappointment. For we know how dearly God loves us, because he has given us the Holy Spirit to fill our hearts with his love" (Romans 5:3-5 NLT).

Notes — Week Two

Week Three

HOPE IN
WHO HE IS

Days 13–18

Day Thirteen

HOPE IN THE LORD

Why are you in despair, O my soul? And
why have you become disturbed within
me? Hope in God, for I shall again
praise Him for the help of His presence.

PSALM 42:5

I t is always too soon to give up. When you feel as though your life
is over and despair threatens to crush your heart, speak to your soul
with the words of the psalmist. "Why are you in despair, O my soul?
And why have you become disturbed within me? Hope in God, for I
shall again praise Him for the help of His presence" (Psalm 42:5). Days
will come when you will need to literally speak (declare) the promises
of God to yourself, to instruct your very heart and soul. The writer of
Psalm 42 was in such desperation that tears were flowing day and night.
Have you ever been in a place like that?

I remember a time when I was in such despair that I found myself
in tears, crying throughout the day. A change in our life and profession
had become a devastating obstacle to me. I was really struggling with
letting go of the life I knew and loved. I could truly relate to the words

of the psalmist: "I am so troubled that I cannot speak" (Psalm 77:4). As I began living in the Psalms, I spoke the promises I discovered to my own heart and soul. The greatest promises that turned my heart from despair to hope were those that told me who God is. I felt as though I had lost the smile of God, like David, who cried out, "How long will You hide Your face from me?" (Psalm 13:1). I eventually realized God loved me and was sovereign and in perfect control. As I turned my heart and mind to the truth of who God is, I was able to surrender the past in order to embrace what God was doing in the present and what He wanted to do in the future. I began to see that God wanted me to have "endured as seeing Him who is unseen," just as Moses did (Hebrews 11:27).

I have discovered that we should never look at God through our feelings and circumstances. Octavius Winslow rightly asserts, "We blindly interpret the symbols of his providence because we so imperfectly read the engravings of his heart."[1] Corrie ten Boom used to quote the following words to help others learn how to see from God's point of view:

> My life is but a weaving between my God and me.
> I do not choose the colors, he worketh steadily.
> Ofttimes he weaveth sorrow, and I in foolish pride,
> Forget he sees the upper, and I the underside.
> Not till the loom is silent and the shuttles cease to fly,
> Will God unroll the canvas and explain the reason why.
> The dark threads are as needful in the skillful weaver's hand,
> As the threads of gold and silver in the pattern he has planned.[2]

The tragedies and traumas of life often appear to us as the dark threads and twisted knots of the underside of a weaving. But if, somehow, we can see the upper side of the weaving, the true picture of who God is, what He does, and what He says, we can move from despair to hope, **H**olding **O**n with **P**atient **E**xpectation. What will help you move from despair to hope? Meet God through His Word, the Bible, and transfer what you see into your feelings and circumstances. When you approach God through His Word, your heart and soul will be dramatically transformed.

Seeing your life as God's weaving will remind you that...

- God, in His infinite wisdom, has a design in mind. "I know the plans that I have for you" (Jeremiah 29:11).

- God is sovereign, the Master Weaver. "He…is the blessed and only Sovereign, the King of kings and Lord of lords" (1 Timothy 6:15).

- God rules over all His design. "Yours, O LORD, is the greatness and the power and the glory and the victory and the majesty, for all that is in the heavens and in the earth is yours…you rule over all" (1 Chronicles 29:11-12 ESV).

- God is aware of and involved in every situation. He holds all things in His hands, including the days He planned for the weaving of your life. "My times are in your hand" (Psalm 31:15).

- Every thread of your life passes through the hand and heart of God, who loves you so much that He gave His own Son, Jesus, to die in your place to pay for your sins. "God is love. In this the love of God was made manifest among us, that God sent his only Son into the world, so that we might live through him" (1 John 1:8-9 ESV).

- God is all-powerful and is at work at all times in your life, weaving together the dark, gold, and silver threads. "And we know that God causes all things to work together for good to those who love God, to those who are called according to His purpose" (Romans 8:28).

Speak these scriptural truths about God to your heart and soul. When you rest on the promises of God in His Word, your heart and soul will know something completely different from what your feelings are saying to you—truth rather than lies, facts rather than fiction, objective reality rather than imagined fantasy. You may be weeping. You may be grieving. You will probably not be merrily skipping through a field of flowers in your life, oblivious to the pain and sorrow you are experiencing. However, like Jeremiah, whose face was often wet with tears, you will still be able to say, "The Lord is my portion, says my soul, therefore I have hope in Him" (Lamentations 3:24).

You will find hope in the promises of God revealed in the names of God. "The name of the LORD is a strong tower; the righteous runs into it and is safe" (Proverbs 18:10). The names of God will help you trust the promise. "Those who know Your name will put their trust in You, for You, O LORD, have not forsaken those who seek You" (Psalm 9:10). When God lets you know what His name is, He is revealing vital information about His character. Learn as much as you can about the names of God, perhaps using a Bible dictionary or encyclopedia.

- *Elohim.* This is the first name of God found in the Bible (Genesis 1:1). The form of the word is plural, pointing to the triune God, and expresses the majesty and almightiness of God. He, Elohim, wants to be your goal and aspiration. He is what life is all about.

- *Adonai.* This name of God means Lord, Master, Owner (Judges 6:15). This name of God reveals that He is worthy of your loyalty, love, and surrender. The name of Adonai encourages you to say to Him, "I surrender all."

- *Jehovah.* This personal name of God is found in the Bible at least 6800 times (Exodus 3:13-16). It means "I am." God is everything you need for every circumstance of life. This name encourages you to draw near to your Lord and depend on Him.

- *Jehovah Sabaoth.* This name means "Lord of hosts" and reveals to you that your Lord is the commander of the armies and will fight for you (1 Samuel 1:3). He is the king of all heaven and earth. This is an encouragement especially when earthly evil seems to have the upper hand. Always remember He is the Lord of hosts, and your battles belong to Him.

- *Jehovah Nissi.* This name means "the Lord my banner" (Exodus 17:15). He is the flag you fly in the battles of life to give you hope and encouragement in the battle.

- *Jehovah Rapha.* This name, meaning "the Lord who heals," encourages you to run to your Great Physician, who can heal physical, emotional, and spiritual affliction (Exodus 15:2-6).

- *Jehovah Raah.* God is "the Lord my Shepherd" (Psalm 23). This name of God encourages you to entrust all your cares to your Shepherd, who loves and watches over you.

• *Jehovah Shammah.* This name of God means "the Lord is there" and reminds you that He is always with you (Ezekiel 48:35). This name assures you that He will never leave you, forsake you, or abandon you. You are never alone.

• *Jehovah Tsidkenu.* This name means "the Lord our righteousness" and reveals to you that He is your standard of what is right and true, and He is the One who can make you righteous (Jeremiah 23:6).

• *Jehovah Jireh.* This name of God means "the Lord will provide" and encourages you to run to Him with all your needs (Genesis 22:14). Knowing He is Jehovah Jireh assures you that He is supplier for your deepest need.

• *Jehovah Shalom.* This name of God means "the Lord is peace" and encourages you to run to Him when you need peace (Judges 6:24). Knowing He is Jehovah Shalom assures you that He is the source of peace.

• *El Shaddai.* This name means "God Almighty" (Genesis 17:1-2). God is all-sufficient for you—this name is the promise that God is enough.

• *El Elyon.* This name means "the Most High God" and expresses His sovereignty, majesty, and preeminence (Genesis 14:19). Knowing He is El Elyon encourages you to trust Him and surrender to Him in your circumstance because you know He is sovereign.

• *El Roi.* This name of God means "the God who sees" and was originally revealed in Hagar's desperate circumstance (Genesis 16:13). Knowing He is El Roi helps you remember that even though no one else may see or understand your trial, He sees and knows and understands all you are going through.

After you have explored the names of God, use *Nave's Topical Bible* to study God's character and attributes. One of the best places in the Bible to find promises about His character is in the Psalms. Choose any psalm and write out everything you learn about God. Then write out everything you see about how the psalmist responded to God. This will help you understand how to apply the promise about His character.

For example, in Psalm 46:1-2, you learn that God is your refuge, God is your strength, and God is a very present help in trouble. How did the psalmist respond? He said, "Therefore we will not fear." This promise encourages you to be courageous because He is your present help in your trouble. To experience more of the promises in the Psalms, you may wish to study one of the eight-week books of quiet times on Psalms available from Quiet Time Ministries: *A Heart That Hopes in God* or *Pilgrimage of the Heart*.

It is imperative in our study of who God is that we see Him as He really is, not as we wish Him to be.

> Without doubt, the mightiest thought the mind can entertain is the thought of God, and the weightiest word in any language is its word for God...That our idea of God correspond as nearly as possible to the true being of God is of immense importance to us...A right conception of God is basic not only to systematic theology but to practical Christian living as well...The man who comes to a right belief about God is relieved of ten thousand temporal problems, for he sees at once that these have to do with matters which at the most cannot concern him for very long; but even if the multiple burdens of time may be lifted from him, the one mighty single burden of eternity begins to press down upon him with a weight more crushing than all the woes of the world piled one upon another. That mighty burden is his obligation to God. It includes an instant and lifelong duty to love God with every power of mind and soul, to obey Him perfectly, and to worship Him acceptably.[3]

Over the years I have collected many books on God's character. The truths in these books have helped me look at God as He really is rather than how I think or feel He is or should be. My favorites include *Knowing God* by J.I. Packer, *The Knowledge of the Holy* by A.W. Tozer, *The Existence and Attributes of God* by Stephen Charnock, *The God of all Comfort* by Hannah Whitall Smith, *Lord, I Want to Know You* by Kay Arthur, and *The Sovereignty of God* by A.W. Pink. I encourage you to put together your own collection of books that you can return to again and again to help you "set your mind on the things above, not on the things that are on earth" (Colossians 3:2).

When you see God as He really is, the greatest result will be praise from your heart. You are, by the grace and mercy of God, lifted above your circumstances and able to see and experience God. And you will worship Him as your soul soars on the wings of hope from the promises of God. Hannah Whitall Smith says this:

> Things look very different according to the standpoint from which we view them. The caterpillar, as it creeps along the ground, must have a widely different view of the world around it from that which the same caterpillar will have when its wings are developed, and it soars in the air above the very places where once it crawled. And it is a very different aspect from the soul that has *mounted up with wings*. The mountain top may blaze with sunshine when all the valley below is shrouded in fog, and the bird whose wings can carry him high enough may mount at will out of the gloom below into the joy of the sunlight above.[4]

John Bunyan was imprisoned for 12 years because of his faith in Christ and his unwillingness to agree with the authorities' demand to stop preaching. He said that if he was to suffer rightly, he needed to "live upon God that is invisible." The great fruit of what Bunyan saw while in prison was the book he wrote during that time, *The Pilgrim's Progress*, one of the bestselling books of all time. George Whitefield commented on the profound nature of *The Pilgrim's Progress*: "It smells of the prison. It was written when the author was confined in Bedford jail. And ministers never write or preach so well as when under the cross: the Spirit of Christ and of Glory then rests upon them."[5]

You may be in the most difficult time of your life, perhaps even a prison of some kind. Will you learn to "live upon God that is invisible"? When you do, you may give in to Him, but you will not give up. And that will be the evidence that you are **Holding On** with **Patient Expectation**.

My Response

DATE:

KEY VERSE: "Why are you in despair, O my soul? And why have you become disturbed within me? Hope in God, for I shall again praise Him for the help of His presence" (Psalm 42:5).

FOR FURTHER THOUGHT: How does knowing who God is help you have hope? How can you "see Him who is invisible"? What have you learned about God that will help you in your life today? What is the most important truth you learned?

MY RESPONSE:

Day Fourteen

HE IS ABLE

Now to him who is able to do far more
abundantly than all that we ask or
think, according to the power at work
within us, to him be the glory in the
church and in Christ Jesus throughout
all generations, forever and ever. Amen.

EPHESIANS 3:20-21 ESV

od is greater than all our wildest imaginings. Even when you think your life is impossible, it is not impossible to God. Why? Because of the incredible promises in Ephesians 3:20-21. "Now to him who is able to do far more abundantly than all that we ask or think, according to the power at work within us, to him be the glory in the church and in Christ Jesus throughout all generations, forever and ever. Amen" (ESV). Nothing is impossible when you know the Lord. These promises about your God can meet your need in any circumstance in your life: fear, sin, suffering, weakness, loss, or change. They are sufficient for all the twists and turns, traumas and devastations of life. Just when you least expect it, God can surprise you with something that never entered your mind, and therefore, you can hope in Him.

Annie Johnson Flint lost her parents before she was six years old and was adopted by a childless couple in New Jersey. To her great pleasure, she discovered she could write poetry at the age of nine, and before she turned twelve, she was putting her poems to music. Although she dreamed of becoming a composer and a concert pianist, she was stricken with crippling arthritis at the age of fourteen, forcing her into a world of poetical artistry. She once said that writing verse was so easy that it never seemed like work, and for 40 years she "endured as seeing Him who is invisible" (Hebrews 11:27 ESV).

A visitor walking into Annie's room would observe nine soft pillows arranged on the bed, cushioning her sensitive, pain-ridden body. Just going to bed at night was a distress for one who endured such pain and suffering. She lived in her wheelchair, but her real life was in God. Her verse carries no hint of self-pity, no defiant question, no negative complaint about the will of God, merely a radiant faith, a joy of life, praise and thanksgiving, and a deep love for God. And that is the message of Annie Johnson Flint's life, gloriously free to soar above the things of this world with the wings of faith and hope in His promises.

The promises of Ephesians 3:20-21 contain three powerful truths about God. First, God is able. The Greek word for "able" is *dunamai* and means to possess an adequate and capable power by virtue of one's own ability and resources. Paul is saying that God possesses within Himself absolute power and unlimited resources.

Second, God does far more abundantly than all we ask or think. God is the God of the impossible. The Greek words translated "far more abundantly" point to the greatest abundance, something over and above and extraordinary. In other words, there is no limit to what God can do in your life. He can do more than the greatest request we ever make to Him in prayer. He can do more than any thought we have. Our greatest idea, our greatest imagining, and our best resolution is nothing compared to what God can do. This means that God has plans in His mind that we have not imagined.

This seems obvious when we actually say it. However, our hearts so easily give in to despair because God does not seem to live up to what we are thinking. Why should He? He is greater than our minds. He is the God of the impossible. He is beyond the realm of the deepest and greatest thought any person can have. Regardless of how impossible your situation is to you and to everyone you know, it is not impossible to God. In fact, God is not worried or panicked about you or your situation. He has something in mind for you, a plan and a purpose. He does not always accomplish what we want, but in fact, He will accomplish more than we can imagine. He created the heavens and the earth, so surely He can create something amazing and incredible in your life.

God takes delight in the impossible situation, for He answers it with Himself. That is what His words in Isaiah promise:

> The afflicted and needy are seeking water, but there is none, and their tongue is parched with thirst; I, the LORD will answer them Myself, as the God of Israel I will not forsake them. I will open rivers on the bare heights, and springs in the midst of valleys; I will make the wilderness a pool of water, and the dry land fountains of water. I will put the cedar in the wilderness, the acacia, and the myrtle, and the olive tree; I will place the juniper in the desert, together with the box tree and the cypress, that they may see and recognize, and consider and gain insight as well, that the hand of the LORD has done this, and the Holy One of Israel has created it (Isaiah 41:17-20).

Do you feel as though you are that juniper in the desert? Are you in a wilderness right now? God can bring great glory to Himself in your wilderness experience. Listen to God's words in Hosea and hold them close to your heart: "But then I will win her back once again. I will lead her into the desert and speak tenderly to her there. I will return her vineyards to her and transform the Valley of Trouble into a gateway of hope" (Hosea 2:14-15 NLT). Your valley of trouble can become the place of hope. Why? Because your Lord is able and He is the God of the impossible. Jesus said, "With people it is impossible, but not with God; for all things are possible with God" (Mark 10:27). Even when Jesus was praying in the garden of Gethsemane in His darkest hour, He prayed, "Abba Father! All things are possible for You; remove this cup from Me; yet not My will, but what You will" (Mark 14:36). In Jesus' prayer you see perfect belief blended with perfect surrender, an assurance that what

God can and will do is greater than all we ask or think. And in fact, God worked the greatest miracle of all because in the death of Jesus on the cross, the penalty of sin was paid, and eternal life became possible for you and me. A work beyond human imagination was transacted on the cross, one that was powerful and effective for all time and eternity.

Third, in the promises of Ephesians 3:20-21, God accomplishes His will according to the power that is at work within us. If you know Christ as your personal Savior, you are indwelt by God Himself through the Holy Spirit. That means that even if you feel inadequate for what you face in life, God who lives in you is all-powerful and all-sufficient for every circumstance. He is enough for everything that comes your way. These words take on new meaning when you realize that Paul was writing them from his own impossible situation—he was in prison. And yet he knew that God was able, God could do the impossible, and God lived in him.

Shortly after Dallas Theological Seminary was founded in 1924, it almost closed its doors, facing bankruptcy. At noon on the day of fore-closure, the founders of the school met in the president's office to pray that God would provide the necessary funds to pay off the creditors. Harry Ironside prayed in his refreshingly candid way, "Lord we know that the cattle on a thousand hills are Thine. Please sell some of them and send us the money." Just about that time, a tall Texan in boots and an open-collared shirt strolled into the business office. "Howdy" he said to the secretary. "I just sold two carloads of cattle in Fort Worth. I've been trying to make a business deal go through, but it just won't work. I feel God wants me to give this money to the seminary. I don't know if you need it or not, but here's the check." The secretary took the check and timidly tapped on the door of the prayer meeting. Dr. Lewis Sperry Chafer, the founder and president of the school, answered and took the check from her hand. When he looked at the amount, he was amazed to see that it was for the exact sum of the debt. Then he realized the name on the check was that of the cattleman. Turning to Dr. Ironside, he said, "Harry, God sold the cattle."

Maybe you need God to sell some cattle for you today. But maybe your need is even more complex and convoluted than a financial one. Only God knows the real needs of your life. Write the check on this powerful promise. Hope in Him today, for He "is able to do far more abundantly than all that we ask or think, according to the power at work within us" (Ephesians 3:20-21).

I know not, but God knows;
Oh, blessed rest from fear!
All my unfolding days
To Him are plain and clear.

Each anxious, puzzled "why?"
From doubt or dread that grows,
Finds answer in this thought:
I know not, but He knows.

I cannot, but God can;
Oh, balm for all my care!
The burden that I drop
His hand will lift and bear.

Though eagle pinions tire,
I walk where once I ran,
This is my strength to know
I cannot, but He can.

I see not, but God sees;
Oh, all-sufficient light!
My dark and hidden way
To Him is always bright.

My strained and peering eyes
May close in restful ease,
And I in peace may sleep;
I see not, but He sees.[1]

ANNIE JOHNSON FLINT

My Response

DATE:

KEY VERSE: "Now to him who is able to do far more abundantly than all that we ask or think, according to the power at work within us, to him be the glory in the church and in Christ Jesus throughout all generations, forever and ever. Amen" (Ephesians 3:20-21 ESV).

FOR FURTHER THOUGHT: How do the promises in Ephesians 3:20-21 encourage you and give you hope today? How did Annie Johnson Flint's life encourage you?

MY RESPONSE:

Day Fifteen

THE EXACT
EXPLANATION
OF GOD

*No one has seen God at any time; the
only begotten God who is in the bosom
of the Father, He has explained Him.*

JOHN 1:18

‿❧

I f you want to know what God is like, look at Jesus. He is the exact explanation of God. John said, "No one has seen God at any time; the only begotten God who is in the bosom of the Father, He has *explained* Him" (John 1:18). The writer of Hebrews tells us that God "has spoken to us in His Son, whom He appointed heir of all things, through whom also He made the world. And He is the radiance of His glory and the *exact* representation of His nature, and upholds all things by the word of His power" (Hebrews 1:2-3). The Greek word translated "exact representation" is *charakter* and implies that Jesus is the exact image and perfect expression of God's essence.

I was in a business center one day, and as I headed for the copy machine, I overheard a man telling a group of people all about God. Of course, that piqued my interest. I listened. To my horror, he was giving them ideas that were not scriptural. "God is impersonal," he said flatly, "He's too busy to communicate with us." I immediately stepped forward and said, "Wait a minute. That's not true." All eyes landed on me. Now everyone in the center was listening. I said, "God is exactly the opposite of what you are telling everyone. He loves you and wants a personal relationship with you." This man responded curtly by saying, "Oh no, you're wrong. God is too busy for us." And he left. Obviously, this man was basing his beliefs entirely on his own thoughts not on what the Bible teaches. And that is where many people err. They form their thoughts and beliefs according to what they have heard somewhere, what they are thinking and feeling at the moment, or what seems to be true.

When interpreting who God is, we must look at His own revelation about Himself in the Bible. What we think or feel or what someone else thinks can never be the authority, standard, or measure of our belief. God's Word alone must be the authority for what we think and believe. When we open the pages of the Bible, we immediately discover that this Jesus, who walked on earth more than two thousand years ago, was more than a man. He claimed to be God through His actions and His words. And in the end, He was crucified not for what He did but for who He claimed to be. When the high priest asked Him, "Are You the Christ, the Son of the Blessed One?" He replied, "I am; and you shall see the Son of Man sitting at the right hand of power and coming with the clouds of heaven" (Mark 14:62). The high priest responded by tearing his clothes, indicating that he considered Jesus' words as a claim to be God and blasphemy (Mark 14:63-64).

When Jesus was hanging on the cross, He cried out three words that defined His mission: "It is finished" (John 19:30). He came to earth to die to satisfy the justice and righteousness of God on our behalf, that we might receive forgiveness of sins and inherit eternal life. This is a fact that is not only taught in the New Testament but prophesied hundreds of years earlier in the Old Testament:

> But the Lord was pleased to crush Him, putting Him to grief; if He would render Himself as a guilt offering, He will see His offspring, He will prolong His days, and the good

pleasure of the LORD will prosper in His hand. As a result of the anguish of His soul, He will see it and be satisfied; by His knowledge the Righteous One, My Servant, will justify the many, as He will bear their iniquities (Isaiah 53:10-11).

This is a prophecy of One who would come on behalf of God—the promised Messiah. Jesus was and is the One. And according to John, He has explained God and is God, the second Person of the Trinity.

We learn in the Bible that God is a triune God: God the Father, God the Son, and God the Holy Spirit. We first see this in Genesis where God is revealed as plural—"Then God said, 'Let Us make man in Our image, according to Our likeness'" (Genesis 1:26). The triune God was involved in creation. "In the beginning God (the plural noun *Elohim*) created the heavens and the earth" (Genesis 1:1). We see that God the Father spoke creation into being (Genesis 1:3). The Spirit of God was "moving over the surface of the waters" (Genesis 1:2). John reveals something powerful about Jesus, the second Person of the triune God: "He was in the world, *and the world was made through Him,* and the world did not know Him" (John 1:10). Then John speaks of Jesus in John 1:18 when he says, "He has explained Him." Jesus is the exact explanation of God. Look very carefully at Jesus, and you can know and understand who God is, what He does, and what He says.

Just think about how your God has revealed Himself to you. He does not play coy, hide, and remain distant. Instead, He has given you every provision to become intimate with Him in a vibrant, powerful relationship. He personally came to earth in the incarnation of Jesus so that you might see and touch Him.

What was from the beginning, what we have heard, what we have seen with our eyes, what we have looked at and touched with our hands, concerning the Word of Life—and the life was manifested, and we have seen and testify and proclaim to you the eternal life, which was with the Father and was manifested to us—what we have seen and heard we proclaim to you also, so that you too may have fellowship with us; and indeed our fellowship is with the Father, and with His Son Jesus Christ (1 John 1:1-3).

You have the written record of Jesus found in the Bible. And now the Bible is in your hands, to open and discover who God is by coming to know the Lord Jesus Christ personally in an intimate relationship. He says to you, "Behold, I stand at the door and knock; if anyone hears My voice and opens the door, I will come in to him and will dine with him, and he with Me" (Revelation 3:20). Will you open that door and commune with Him today? If so, you are going to discover the Lord in a way that you have never known Him before, and you will experience what the two men on the road to Emmaus experienced when they met Jesus and dined with Him: "Were not our hearts burning within us while He was speaking to us on the road, while He was explaining the Scriptures to us?" (Luke 24:32). May your heart burn with a contagious love for Jesus that spreads to the world.

DATE:

KEY VERSE: "No one has seen God at any time; the only begotten God who is in the bosom of the Father, He has explained Him" (John 14:18).

FOR FURTHER THOUGHT: What impresses you the most about Jesus today?

MY RESPONSE:

JESUS WEPT

When Jesus therefore saw her weeping,
and the Jews who came with her also
weeping, He was deeply moved in
spirit and was troubled...Jesus wept.

JOHN 11:33-35

Jesus feels the emotion of your heart. His great love for you moves Him to a deep, intimate involvement with you. Two of the greatest words in the Bible are those found in the Gospel of John when Mary and Martha summoned Jesus in their great crisis—the death of their brother, Lazarus. The text tells us that Jesus loved Mary, Martha, and Lazarus (John 11:5). And when Jesus arrived at Lazarus' tomb, He saw Mary and others weeping, and "He was deeply moved in spirit and was troubled" (John 11:33). Jesus experienced a deep emotion—He was visibly upset and angry (according to the Greek rendering) and moved in His heart to the point of tears. As John tells us, "Jesus wept" (John 11:35).

This event reveals a profound promise for our own suffering—when we weep, the Lord Jesus is emotionally moved and weeps with us. Because He is the exact explanation of God, we see that the heart of

God is more than we thought or imagined. He experiences emotion and feels our pain. When He saw those whom He loved weeping, He wept. When you weep, He weeps. Having a friend weep with you is one thing, but knowing the Lord Jesus weeps with you is quite another. When He experiences your pain with you, His indescribable empathy and intimacy brings true comfort. F.B. Meyer points out that "they are not tears of weak sentiment, but of noble pathos that hastens to help with divine sufficiency."[1] God is, indeed, the Father of mercies and God of all comfort (2 Corinthians 1:3). The psalmist experienced this facet of God's character and wrote, "You have taken account of my wanderings; put my tears in Your bottle. Are they not in Your book?" (Psalm 56:8). Your tears mean so much to the Lord that He actually has a bottle for them and takes note of them in a book that belongs to Him. In this verse, you see how intensely personal your God is and how involved He is in the events of your life. "The Lord has heard the voice of my weeping" (Psalm 6:8).

> Tears of grief and tears of joy often mingle together in a single moment of enhanced vision, endowing us with new eyes that discern traces of the God who suffers with us silently in the pure vulnerability and power of divine love. There is comfort in such tears. They bring fresh understanding that God is nearby, sharing to the full our humanity in all its bitterness and blessedness.[2]

You can know that in God's time, His personal, intimate involvement in your life will bring about a dramatic change: "Weeping may last for the night, but a shout of joy comes in the morning" (Psalm 30:5).

We see in the raising of Lazarus that the Lord was "deeply moved" (the Greek word *embrimaomai* means anger) by the effects of sin and evil and a fallen world. Sin and death are the true sources of Jesus' anger at Lazarus' death. What else could have provoked such deep emotion? He surely was not angry at the sorrow of His friends—He wept along with them. And if He saw hypocrisy in the Jewish mourners, would it have provoked Him to such deep and moving anger? It could have contributed to His deep emotion, but surely it isn't the complete source for the anger. For a brief moment we are given a glimpse into the heart of the

Giver of life, the Designer of all perfection, the Creator of the universe coming face-to-face with what He hates the most—evil, sin, suffering, and death. Out of *that* heart, the Father was willing to send His only Son, Jesus, to set right the original sin of Adam.

> Through one man sin entered into the world, and death through sin, and so death spread to all men…As through one transgression there resulted condemnation to all men, even so through one act of righteousness there resulted justification of life to all men…so through the obedience of the One the many will be made righteous…as sin reigned in death, even so grace would reign through righteousness to eternal life through Jesus Christ our Lord (Romans 5:12-21).

When Jesus knew Lazarus had died, Jesus must have emotionally faced the purpose of His mission: to save the world. When God sees His people in trouble, He wants to rescue and deliver them. The psalmist said, "God is to us a God of deliverances; and to GOD the Lord belong escapes from death" (Psalm 68:20). What greater deliverance, what greater rescue do God's people need than deliverance from sin and death? When Jesus met Martha after Lazarus' death, He said, "I am the resurrection and the life; he who believes in Me will live even if he dies, and everyone who lives and believes in Me will never die" (John 11:25-26). He knew He had come to earth to die so that the sting of death (eternal separation from God) could be destroyed forever. His death on the cross would accomplish what only He could accomplish and what man could never do for himself: forgiveness of sins, justification of life to all men, righteousness, and eternal life.

Look closely at God's heart here. No human being can feel such incredibly intense sorrow for the devastating effects of sin as does God Himself. Our sin cost Him everything—the life of His dear Son, Jesus. The result is a gift of grace to us—unmerited favor—if we come to Him and receive it. We are completely undeserving, and yet we are recipients of God's grand favor. What was the cost of that favor? Who paid the price? It cost the life of Jesus. He paid the complete and ultimate price—death on the cross.

Isaiah gives us a deeper view of the sacrifice of Jesus, and we must study this image if we are to realize all the color and texture in the true picture. Here is what really happened:

> The LORD was pleased to crush Him, putting Him to grief; if He would render Himself as a guilt offering, He will see His offspring...As a result of the anguish of His soul, He will see it and be satisfied; by His knowledge the Righteous One, My Servant, will justify the many, as He will bear their iniquities...Because He poured out Himself to death, and was numbered with the transgressors; yet He Himself bore the sin of many, and interceded for the transgressors (Isaiah 53:10-12).

Think about it. God the Father, was "pleased" to crush Jesus, putting Him to grief, if Jesus would give Himself up as a guilt offering. God experienced "anguish" (Hebrew, *amal,* or distress) in His soul, but He saw the offering of Jesus, and that sacrifice satisfied the demands of His holiness and righteousness. Jesus gave Himself willingly for you. He loves you; He hates evil, sin, suffering, and death; and He desires to set you free from it all.

What did Jesus experience on the cross? Understanding His suffering will help you immeasurably when you are going through any difficulties, sorrow, suffering, or loss in your life. In day 15 we saw Jesus' mission described in Isaiah 53:3-5. These words also reveal the true experience of the cross:

> He was despised and forsaken of men, a man of sorrows and acquainted with grief; and like one from whom men hide their face. He was despised, and we did not esteem Him. Surely our griefs He Himself bore, and our sorrows He carried; yet we ourselves esteemed Him stricken, smitten of God, and afflicted. But He was pierced through for our transgressions, He was crushed for our iniquities; the chastening for our well-being fell upon Him, and by His scourging we are healed.

Read those verses again and let them sink deep into your heart. These are promises for you to remember when you face any difficulty. You can know Jesus is a man of sorrows and has experienced grief. This is a great comfort when we grieve—our Lord knows our pain. If you have ever been despised or forsaken, you can know Jesus has experienced hatred and abandonment. And when He was on the cross, He bore our griefs and carried our sorrows. Every pain you have ever felt, every loss you have ever experienced, and every difficulty you have ever suffered, however small or large, He experienced while hanging on the cross. No wonder He suffered such agony on the cross. Jesus' sufferings have been rightly referred to as His *passion*.

No human being could effect such a miraculous oneness and identification with another human being. But according to Isaiah 53, Jesus became one with you, literally identifying with you in the deepest, most desperate part of your being. God allowed Jesus to carry and bear all that you have, all that you are, and all that you will ever experience in your life. He not only carried your suffering but also bore your sin. "He made Him who knew no sin to be sin on our behalf, so that we might become the righteousness of God in Him" (2 Corinthians 5:21).

In light of the cross, no wonder Paul exclaimed in Romans 11:33, "Oh, the depth of the riches both of the wisdom and knowledge of God! How unsearchable are His judgments and unfathomable His ways!"

This is intimacy and union with Christ at its very highest level. Paul tells us that we are united with Christ in His death and resurrection (Romans 6:5) and that we are "in Him" (see Ephesians 1). When He died, we died. When He rose from the dead, we were granted the keys that unlock the door to resurrection life and eternity with Him. What a comfort and what a joy to know such a union with our Lord. We experience oneness with Christ by faith according to what we know from the Bible, and we are accorded a palpable sense of union as we walk daily with our Lord. But Jesus experienced an infinitely deeper and more intimate union with you while hanging on the cross. He knows you through and through—better than you know yourself. And He loves you still. He Himself said, "Greater love has no one than this, that one lay down his life for his friends" (John 15:13).

When we suffer because of evil in the world, we are experiencing what the Bible calls "the fellowship of His sufferings." Paul said, "More than that, I count all things as loss in view of the surpassing value of knowing Christ Jesus my Lord, for whom I have suffered the loss of all things, and count them but rubbish so that I may gain Christ…that I may know Him and the power of His resurrection, and the fellowship of His sufferings" (Philippians 3:8,10). The Greek word for "fellowship" is *koinonia* and refers to sharing, participation, and communion. The Lord Jesus, who knows all things, is ever mindful that in your suffering you are experiencing a communion with Him, a participation with Him in His very deepest pain. The fellowship of His sufferings is a privileged intimacy that you have been granted for this moment of time until you step into eternity. Paul says, "Momentary light affliction is producing for us an eternal weight of glory far beyond all comparison" (2 Corinthians 4:17).

And what do you have to look forward to in eternity? Ultimately, you are going to be set free from every effect of sin. When you stand face-to-face with your Lord in eternity, He will wipe away every tear from your eyes, and "there will no longer be any death; there will no longer be any mourning, or crying, or pain; the first things have passed away" (Revelation 21:4). In addition, "there will no longer be any curse" (Revelation 22:3), you will serve Him, you will see His face, and you will reign forever and ever (Revelation 22:4-5). You can know that these words are faithful and true, according to Revelation 22:6. That means you can count on these promises and write a check to draw upon your spiritual bank account. These may well be the greatest promises in the Bible and the source of infinite hope.

My Response

DATE:

KEY VERSE: "Jesus wept" (John 11:35).

FOR FURTHER THOUGHT: What does the fact that Jesus wept mean to you? After reading so many promises today, what encouraged you the most? Did you learn something new that gave you insight into God's heart? How will what you have read give you hope?

MY RESPONSE:

Day Seventeen

HE IS YOUR
WONDERFUL
COUNSELOR

*For a child will be born to us, a son will
be given to us; And the government will
rest on His shoulders; And His name will
be called Wonderful Counselor, Mighty
God, Eternal Father, Prince of Peace.*

ISAIAH 9:6

The Lord has just the right answer for your every situation. When you do not know what to do or which way to go, rely on the Lord's promise to be your Wonderful Counselor. Isaiah tells us, "For a child will be born to us, a son will be given to us: And the government will rest on His shoulders; and His name will be called Wonderful Counselor, Mighty God, Eternal Father, Prince of Peace" (Isaiah 9:6). "Wonderful" in Hebrew *(pele)* describes something that is absolutely amazing, and "Counselor" in Hebrew *(ya'ats)* means wise adviser. When taken together, the whole is greater than the sum of its parts. "Wonderful Counselor" moves from the realm of merely incredible to eternally miraculous. Our Wonderful Counselor provides just the right answer for you in the heat of your trial, testing, or suffering.

David, the king of God's people, regularly sought earthly counsel (1 Chronicles 27:33). However, what set David apart from other leaders was his practice of asking the Lord for guidance. When David was faced with the threat of his enemies, the Philistines, he "inquired of the Lord, saying, 'Shall I go and attack these Philistines?'" (1 Samuel 23:2). The Lord, his Wonderful Counselor, saw David's open heart and gave him a specific answer—in this case, to attack the Philistines. When David learned of his army's fear, he ran again to God and asked Him for help. And again, the Lord advised him (1 Samuel 23:4). Just as God was with David, He is always there for you.

David's practice of prayer is a great example of how to take advantage of the promise implied in the name "Wonderful Counselor." We must learn to pray. James encourages prayer in the heat of trials and testing: "But if any of you lacks wisdom, let him ask of God, who gives to all generously and without reproach, and it will be given to him" (James 1:5). Matthew Henry emphasizes the importance of asking for wisdom in the midst of our suffering:

> We should not pray so much for the removal of an affliction as for wisdom to make a right use of it. And who is there that does not want wisdom under any great trials or exercises to guide him in his judging of things, in the government of his own spirit and temper, and in the management of his affairs? To be wise in trying times is a special gift of God, and to Him we must seek for it.[1]

God may not always answer in the way we expect, but He will give us wisdom according to His promises in Isaiah 9:6 and James 1:5. J.I. Packer points out that "the kind of wisdom that God waits to give to those who ask Him, is a wisdom that will bind us to Himself, a wisdom that will find expression in a spirit of faith and a life of faithfulness."[2]

I remember a particularly traumatic day when I had to give a very serious meassage to a large group of suffering women at a local church that was undergoing a crisis. I had less than a day to prepare because of the urgency of the hour. I fell before my Lord, my Wonderful Counselor, and asked Him for wisdom. Then, renewed in my spirit, I got up from the floor, dried my eyes, sat down at the computer, and began writing that message. I am still amazed at how quickly the words came to me. Instantly, I knew the passage of Scripture for the message. Although I had no idea of the intensity of the response, I was confident that I had God's message for God's people in their dark hour. As a result, I was able to give the message from His Word with the burden of the Lord pressed in on my heart, producing a confident hope in Him. Later that day, after I gave that message, I was in a Christian bookstore. A woman walked up to me with tears in her eyes and said, "Catherine, that was quite a message. It was very powerful and moving." I said, "Well, you can thank the Lord because it was entirely from Him."

In this name of the Lord Jesus, Wonderful Counselor, you see the matchless wisdom of God. He is all-wise (Romans 16:27) and longs to counsel you with His wisdom. He says, "I will instruct you and teach you in the way which you should go; I will counsel you with My eye upon you" (Psalm 32:8). You can know that Christ is "the power of God and the wisdom of God" (1 Corinthians 1:24). Here is the great promise: "You are in Christ Jesus, who became to us wisdom from God, and righteousness and sanctification, and redemption" (1 Corinthians 1:30). When God gives you wisdom, He is giving you great wealth (Romans 11:33). In fact, God bestowed great favor on King Solomon because, although he could have asked for any earthly possessions, he asked God for wisdom instead (1 Kings 3:10). The Greek word for "wisdom" is *sophia* and means deep knowledge, understanding, and moral insight. I like to think of wisdom as applied truth because "wisdom is vindicated by her deeds" (Matthew 11:19). Wisdom knows what to do with the knowledge God gives you. Take time to meditate on these verses about wisdom and write out your insights.

Wisdom gives you understanding (1 Kings 4:29).

Wisdom comes from God (1 Kings 5:12; Proverbs 2:6).

Wisdom enables you to carry out what God has given you to do (Ezra 7:25).

Wisdom contains secrets and takes you into the deep things of God (Job 11:6-7).

Wisdom is of great worth (Job 28:18).

Wisdom is found in the mouths of the righteous (Psalm 37:30).

Wisdom is expressed in wisely numbering our days and making the most of our time (Psalm 90:12).

God shaped His creation in wisdom (Psalm 104:24).

Wisdom is discovered by fearing the Lord (Psalm 111:10).

Wisdom is given to the upright (Proverbs 2:7).

Wisdom comes into your heart (Proverbs 2:10).

Wisdom requires attention (Proverbs 5:1).

Wisdom is given to the humble (Proverbs 11:2).

Wisdom rests in the heart of one who has understanding (Proverbs 14:33).

Wisdom is like a fountain (Proverbs 18:4).

Wisdom comes from listening to advice and accepting instruction (Proverbs 19:20).

Wisdom is part of effective guidance (Proverbs 20:18; 24:6).

Wisdom gives you a future and a hope (Proverbs 24:14).

Wisdom leads to deliverance (Proverbs 28:26).

Wisdom is a means of great gain (Ecclesiastes 2:13).

Wisdom helps you to succeed (Ecclesiastes 10:10).

Wisdom comes from the Holy Spirit (Isaiah 11:2).

Wisdom is justified by her deeds (Matthew 11:19).

Wisdom from God is so great that your adversaries cannot withstand it or contradict it (Luke 21:15).

Wisdom comes to the mature (1 Corinthians 2:6).

Wisdom gives you the riches of His grace (Ephesians 1:8).

Wisdom fills you with the knowledge of His will (Colossians 1:9).

Wisdom contains treasures and is found in Christ (Colossians 2:3).

Wisdom is from above, and is first pure, then peaceable, gentle, reasonable, full of mercy and good fruits, unwavering, and without hypocrisy (James 3:17).

You may be wondering how the Lord can speak to you and give you wisdom in your difficult situation. The answer is to open the pages of the Bible, the Word of God. "The law of the LORD is perfect, restoring the soul; the testimony of the LORD is sure, making wise the simple" (Psalm 19:7). Paul told Timothy that the Word of God was "profitable for teaching, for reproof, for correction, for training in righteousness; so that the man of God may be adequate, equipped for every good work" (2 Timothy 3:16-17). The Lord will speak to you in His Word and give you exactly the wisdom you need for what you face. You may have to wait for Him to show it to you, but in His perfect timing, He will give you precisely what you need to know. Always remember to ask Him. Never let the words of James 4:2 be true of you: "You do not have because you do not ask." When God answers you with His wisdom in His Word at just the right time in the right circumstances, you will discover that His Word is "like apples of gold in settings of silver" (Proverbs 25:11).

My Response

DATE:

KEY VERSE: "For a child will be born to us, a son will be given to us: And the government will rest on His shoulders; and His name will be called Wonderful Counselor, Mighty God, Eternal Father, Prince of Peace" (Isaiah 9:6).

FOR FURTHER THOUGHT: How do you need your Wonderful Counselor today? What was your favorite truth about wisdom? How has God given you wisdom as you have explored what it means to hope in Him?

MY RESPONSE:

QUIET TIME WEEK THREE: HOPE IN JESUS YOUR SAVIOR

For it was the Father's good pleasure
for all the fullness to dwell in Him,
and through Him to reconcile all
things to Himself, having made peace
through the blood of the cross.

COLOSSIANS 1:19-20

PREPARE YOUR HEART

This week you have been looking at what it means to have hope in the Lord. And you have thought about who the Lord is. Today you are going to look at one of the most life-changing truths about your Lord— He is your Savior. Knowing this truth sets you free from the guilt and condemnation of sin. Oh, what a day it is when you realize your sins are forgiven and your eternal destiny is secure! The message of the gospel never gets old. Ask the Lord to speak to your heart as you sit with Him in your quiet time today.

READ AND STUDY GOD'S WORD

1. Paul wrote a powerful letter to the Colossian church. In the first chapter he wrote about Jesus. Read Colossians 1:13-20 and write out

everything you learn about Jesus. Personalize your observations like this: He purchased my freedom and forgave my sins (Colossians 1:14).

2. Read the following verses and write your insights about being redeemed and forgiven of sins:

Romans 8:1

Ephesians 1:7

Titus 3:5-7

3. If Jesus is your Savior, what are you saved from?

4. If Jesus is your Savior, what hope do you have?

ADORE GOD IN PRAYER

Pray the prayer of David today:

> Search me, O God, and know my heart; Try me and know my anxious thoughts; And see if there be any hurtful way in me, And lead me in the everlasting way (Psalm 139:23-24).

YIELD YOURSELF TO GOD

Could there be a sweeter word in any language than that word "forgiveness," when it sounds in a guilty sinner's ear, like the silver notes of jubilee to the captive Israelite? Blessed, for ever blessed be that dear star of pardon which shines into the condemned cell, and gives the perishing a gleam of hope amid the midnight of despair! Can it be possible that sin, such sin as mine, can be forgiven, forgiven altogether, and for ever? Hell is my portion as a sinner—there is no possibility of my escaping from it while sin remains upon me—can the load of guilt be uplifted, the crimson stain removed? Can the adamantine stones of my prison-house ever be loosed from their mortices, or the doors be lifted from their hinges? Jesus tells me that I may yet be clear. For ever blessed be the revelation of atoning love which not only tells me that pardon is possible, but that it is secured to all who rest in Jesus. I have believed in the appointed propitiation, even Jesus crucified, and therefore my sins are at this moment, and for ever, forgiven by virtue of his substitutionary pains and death. What joy is this! What bliss to be a perfectly pardoned soul! My soul dedicates all her powers to him who of his own unpurchased love became my surety, and wrought out for me redemption through his blood. What riches of grace does free forgiveness exhibit! To forgive at all, to forgive fully, to forgive freely, to forgive for ever! Here is a constellation of wonders; and when I think of how great my sins were, how dear were the precious drops which cleansed me from them, and how gracious was the method by which pardon was sealed home to me, I am in a maze of wondering worshipping affection. I bow before the throne which absolves me, I clasp the cross which delivers me, I serve henceforth all my days the Incarnate God, through whom I am this night a pardoned soul.[1]

CHARLES SPURGEON

ENJOY HIS PRESENCE

Do you know the forgiveness of sins today? Perhaps you have surrendered your life to Jesus and experienced forgiveness of sins, and yet you may still be carrying a load of guilt. Will you draw near to Jesus, your Savior, and confess every sin that comes to your mind, knowing that "if we confess our sins, He is faithful and righteous to forgive us our sins and to cleanse us from all unrighteousness" (1 John 1:9)? You can know that "as far as the east is from the west, so far has He removed our transgressions from us" (Psalm 103:12), and "there is therefore now no condemnation to those who are in Christ Jesus" (Romans 8:1). Those are promises designed to give you hope today.

REST IN HIS LOVE

"He has not dealt with us according to our sins, nor rewarded us according to our iniquities. For as high as the heavens are above the earth, so great is His lovingkindness toward those who fear Him" (Psalm 103:10-11).

Notes — Week Three

Week Four

HOPE IN
WHAT HE DOES

Days 19—24

HE WORKS IN ME

For I am confident of this very thing, that
He who began a good work in you, will
perfect it until the day of Christ Jesus.

PHILIPPIANS 1:6

God promises He will finish the good work He has begun in you. That promise can fill you with hope when you cannot seem to do anything right. Nothing in your life seems to make sense; all is impossible confusion. Paul encouraged the suffering Philippian church, "For I am confident of this very thing, that He who began a good work in you, will perfect it until the day of Christ Jesus" (Philippians 1:6). Others may have given up on you. In fact, maybe *you* have given up on you. But God will never give up on you; He keeps working, and as Eugene Peterson paraphrases in The Message, He "brings to a flourishing finish" the goal He has in mind for you. And what is that ultimate goal? That you become a saint who will reign with Him forever and ever in eternity.

God is, by His very nature, Creator. When He makes His home in you, He initiates a new creation in you that He alone will bring to completion. According to Paul in Colossians 1:13-14, God rescued you from the domain of darkness, transferred you to the kingdom of His beloved Son, Jesus Christ, redeemed you (paid the price for your freedom), and forgave you of all your sins (put them away and delivered you from their power). As a result, you are a new creation in Christ; the old things have passed away, and new things now have come (2 Corinthians 5:17).

I remember sitting in a little cabin, looking out a window at majestic pine trees reaching to the sky, pondering God's creation. Suddenly, a beautiful blue jay landed on one of the pine branches and then easily hopped from branch to branch with wings perfectly designed to carry it upward. As quickly as it had come, it soared skyward into the blue haze. That blue jay was designed by the Master Designer, God, to fly. In the same way, the Master Designer has designed you perfectly to live in a love relationship with Him. You are indwelt by the Holy Spirit, and you are being conformed more and more to the image of Christ (Romans 8:9,29). According to the Bible, you are no longer a human being without hope in the world (Ephesians 2:12); you are a saint (Ephesians 2:19). The word "saint" in the Greek is *hagios* and means you are called out of the world to be set apart, holy, chaste, and pure. You are now in the presence of the living God because He lives in you.

You may be thinking, *I don't feel like a saint. I don't look like a saint. And I certainly don't act like a saint.* Then, dear friend, find hope in this promise: "It is God who is at work in you, both to will and to work for His good pleasure" (Philippians 2:13). That means God is accomplishing a mighty work in you, a transformation, to bring about something magnificent within you that pleases Him.

Kenneth Wuest explains in his notes on Philippians 2:13 how God works in us:

> The words "to will" are the translation of a Greek word meaning "to desire," and refer to a desire that comes from one's emotions rather than from one's reason. It is this desire to do the good pleasure of God that is produced by divine energy in the heart of the saint as he definitely subjects himself to the Holy Spirit's ministry. It is God the Holy Spirit who energizes the saint, making him not only willing,

but actively desirous of doing God's sweet will. But He does not merely leave the saint with the desire to do His will. He provides the necessary power to do it. This we have in the words "to do" [*to work* in the NASB]. The Greek construction implies habit, the habitual doing of God's will.

In verse twelve, we have human responsibility [*work out your salvation* in the NASB], in verse thirteen, divine enablement [*God who is at work in you* in the NASB], a perfect balance which must be kept if the Christian life is to be lived at its best. It is not a *"let go and let God"* affair. It is a *"take hold with God"* business. It is a "mutual co-operation" with the Holy Spirit in an interest and an activity in the things of God. The saint must not merely rest in the Holy Spirit for victory over sin and the production of a holy life. He must in addition to this dependence upon the Spirit, say a positive NO to sin and exert himself to the doing of the right. Here we have that incomprehensible and mysterious interaction between the free will of man and the sovereign grace of God.[1]

Jesus invites you to this mutual cooperation when He says, "Come to Me, all who are weary and heavy-laden, and I will give you rest. Take my yoke upon you and learn from Me, for I am gentle and humble in heart, and you will find rest for your souls. For My yoke is easy and My burden is light" (Matthew 11:28-30). Jesus is inviting you to be His disciple. The yoke symbolizes the decision to submit to His leadership and lordship in your life. The promise of the easy yoke flows out of Jesus' nature—He is gentle and humble in heart. We become pupils of the Lord Jesus Himself, and He promises to teach us in such a way that we will learn from Him. When you take on this easy yoke and learn from Jesus as His disciple, you will see growth and transformation in your life with Him. The Lord wants us to be mature Christians, grown up and living on the solid food of His Word (1 Corinthians 14:20; Hebrews 5:14; 6:1).

John Newton was the son of a commander of a merchant ship. By the time he was 11 he had made six voyages with his father. After his father retired, Newton served on a ship where conditions were so intolerable that he deserted his service. He was captured, publicly flogged, and finally exchanged into service on a slave ship. He became the servant of a slave trader but was rescued by a sea captain who was a friend of his father. John Newton eventually became captain of his own ship, one involved in the slave trade. During a voyage through a violent storm, Newton cried out, "Lord, have mercy upon us." Later, in his cabin, he could not get those words out of his mind and saw that God was reaching out to him in the storm. He surrendered his life to the Lord. After some time he married, gave up his ship and the slave trade, and began to educate himself. He taught himself Latin, Greek, and Hebrew and became friends with the great English evangelist George Whitefield. He eventually became a minister and preached at Olney, England. Another of his friends was the poet William Cowper, with whom he collaborated on several editions of Olney hymns. The most well-known of John Newton's hymns is "Amazing Grace." John Newton is a real-life example of God's amazing grace; his life is a testimony to God's life-changing power at work within us.

When I first received Jesus as my Savior and Lord, I didn't know Him very well, in fact, almost not at all. At the time, I was attending a university known for its parties—and I surely loved parties! But once I entered into a relationship with Christ, I became a new person. I soon found I was more interested in what He had to say to me than living a party life. So I went to the local Christian bookstore and bought a Bible, and to my roommates' surprise, I began reading it. My roommates couldn't believe I was the same person they had known. And I wasn't. I had discovered that God had much to say to me in the Bible and was transforming me on the inside—I actually wanted to please Him! I wanted to know Him and walk with Him and live with Him each day.

Before long I started setting aside a time each day to sit with Him, read my Bible, and talk with Him about what I was reading—my quiet time. I soon discovered that what I read in the Bible called for a response. I could say yes to the Lord or no to Him. Saying yes often meant confessing a sin, getting involved in Bible study, or forgiving a friend who had hurt me. When I said yes, I made progress, and my character began to change. I was not the old Catherine, who lived for herself, but the new Catherine, who lived and walked with the Lord. That is what happens when "God...is at work in you both to will and to work for His good pleasure." We can have the confident assurance that He will continue working in us until we see Him face-to-face. If you are discouraged about your own spiritual progress, write the check on Philippians 1:6 and 2:13 today and begin to embrace the words, trust them, and live them out in your daily life.

Amazing grace, how sweet the sound
That saved a wretch like me.
I once was lost but now am found;
Was blind, but now I see.

'Twas grace that taught my heart to fear,
And grace my fears relieved.
How precious did that grace appear
the hour I first believed.

When we've been there ten thousand years,
Bright shining as the sun,
We've no less days to sing God's praise
Than when we first begun.

JOHN NEWTON

My Response

DATE:

KEY VERSE: "For I am confident of this very thing, that He who began a good work in you, will perfect it until the day of Christ Jesus" (Philippians 1:6).

FOR FURTHER THOUGHT: How does knowing that God is at work in you and will complete that work encourage you today? What is the most important truth you read that gives you hope? Are you making progress as a Christian? How will you know? Have you taken on the yoke of discipleship, and are you learning from Christ?

MY RESPONSE:

Day Twenty

HE INTERCEDES
FOR ME

He always lives to make intercession for them.

HEBREWS 7:25

Jesus carries you into the very throne room of God Himself. He is your Intercessor. The writer of Hebrews tells you that "He always lives to make intercession for them" (Hebrews 7:25). In Romans 8:34 we see that it is Christ Jesus who "also intercedes for us." In this promise is great hope for you in your deepest desperation. Even when you do not know what to ask or cannot find the strength to pray, Jesus brings His prayer for you to the throne of God the Father.

The Greek word translated "intercedes" is *entugchano* and means to direct a petition toward God on behalf of someone. In this case, Jesus is bringing a petition to God on your behalf. Oh, what a promise this is for you! A.B. Simpson says, "In Christ we are presented by our Great High Priest before the throne in our prayers and in our worship, and we are accepted for His sake, even as He Himself is accepted. He hands over the petition in your name, and puts His name on the back; and your prayers to the Father as if He were asking. He is in His very person and character your Representative."[1]

One of my favorite examples of Jesus' intercession is found in Peter's story in Luke 22:31-34. Jesus said to Peter, "Simon, Simon, behold, Satan has demanded permission to sift you like wheat; but I have prayed for you, that your faith may not fail; and you, when once you have turned again, strengthen your brothers." Peter responded by saying his faith would never fail. Jesus, who is greater than our hearts (1 John 3:20), told Peter that he would deny Jesus three times that very day. And, in fact, Peter did deny Jesus three times. Immediately following his denials, the rooster crowed, and Luke 22:61 tells us that "the Lord turned and looked at Peter. And Peter remembered the word of the Lord." Peter wept bitterly at his failure. But oh, how powerful are Jesus' prayers on our behalf. Even when we fail, the Lord's prayers bring us to the other side of that failure. What a day it was when Peter saw the resurrected Lord standing on the beach. Peter threw himself into the sea and swam to shore. Jesus approached him directly and commissioned Peter to follow Him and to be the shepherd who tends His sheep (John 21:9-19). In fact, Peter was a primary leader of the early church, and he was eventually martyred for his faith in Christ. Jesus' prayers held him strong and made him faithful to the end.

Jesus intercedes for you in your temptations, sins, weaknesses, and needs. F.B. Meyer says that "He stands for us with God and for God with us."[2] This means that Jesus is *for you* and is intimately involved *with you*. He does not expect you to carry your sin, but instead, to run to Him with it, confess it, and leave it with Him. According to the promise of 1 John 1:9, "If we confess our sins, He is faithful and righteous to forgive us our sins and to cleanse us from all unrighteousness." He does not expect you to carry your needs as burdens but instead to "cast all your anxiety on him because he cares for you" (1 Peter 5:7 NIV). The writer of Hebrews encourages you with these words: "For we do not have a high priest who cannot sympathize with our weaknesses, but one who has been tempted in all things as we are, yet without sin. Therefore, let us draw near with confidence to the throne of grace, so that we may receive mercy and find grace to help in time of need" (Hebrews 4:15-16). According to Paul in Romans 5:2, we stand in grace, not condemnation. Grace is the unmerited favor of God, **G**od's **R**iches **A**t **C**hrist's **E**xpense. Grace gives you everything you need even when you do not deserve it because of Jesus' ongoing intercession on your behalf. What are you to do with such a promise? How can you write the check when you have done nothing to deserve it? You must accept it from the Lord as a gift. Receive it from Him and then act on it. Live it. Run to Him in every situation and at any time because He is your Intercessor.

He giveth more grace as the burdens grow greater,
He sendeth more strength when the labors increase,
To added afflictions He addeth His mercy,
To multiplied trials His multiplied peace.

When we have exhausted our store of endurance,
When our strength has failed ere the day is half done,
When we reach the end of our hoarded resources,
Our Father's full giving is only begun.

His love has no limit, His grace has no measure,
His power has no boundary known unto men;
For out of His infinite riches in Jesus,
He giveth, and giveth, and giveth again!

ANNIE JOHNSON FLINT

My Response

DATE:

KEY VERSE: "He always lives to make intercession for them" (Hebrews 7:25).

FOR FURTHER THOUGHT: How do you need the intercession of the Lord Jesus today? Will you take your need to Him and receive His grace and mercy?

MY RESPONSE:

Day Twenty-One

HE
STRENGTHENS ME

I can do all things through
Him who strengthens me.

PHILIPPIANS 4:13

God promises to strengthen you in all things. You cannot do the impossible task set before you, but the Lord can. Paul said, "I can do all things through Him who strengthens me" (Philippians 4:13). The Greek word translated "strengthen" is *endunamoo* and points to an equipping with the power necessary to accomplish a task. What is the secret to living the Christian life and running the race set before you? That secret is to be filled with the Holy Spirit and to live in the strength and power of the Lord. This is the promise for you when you feel so weak you have no idea how you can live your life. Your battle cry becomes, "I can't, but He can!"

I have learned to become excited when I am faced with a task that asks for more than I am capable of doing. That's when I know that the Lord wants to do something amazing and incredible through me according to His power and strength. I learned this one day early on in my ministry, when at least a thousand women were scheduled to attend one of my speaking engagements. This would be the largest audience I had spoken to. While eating their wonderful lunch, I wondered how in the world I was actually going to get up on that huge stage and give the message I had agreed by faith to deliver. I admit that I became quite panicked and thought for a brief moment I would just get out of my chair and run out the back door. Then it struck me: *I can't do that. The Lord is asking me to speak to these women.* I repeated the words of Philippians 4:13 silently to the Lord: *"I can do all things through Him who strengthens me." Well Lord, that includes even this event. I can't, but You can. Okay, Lord, I'm going for it.* So when I was introduced, I walked boldly up on the stage and began sharing my message. I sensed a new power come over me and a complete dissipation of the fear. The words came so easily. As I walked back and forth across that stage interacting with faces in the audience, I knew this event had become more than a speaking engagement to me. It was a battle for souls and a war for the spiritual revival of those who were listening. I admit I loved every minute of my time ministering to those women. The Lord had worked in a powerful way that day and taught me something very important—I can't, but He can.

How can we live in the strength of the Lord? By being filled with the Holy Spirit. Paul said, "And do not get drunk with wine, for that is dissipation, but be filled with the Spirit" (Ephesians 5:18). When you are filled with the Holy Spirit, you are controlled and empowered by Jesus Christ. How can you experience His fullness? Simply by confessing your sins (the Lord fills clean vessels) and asking Him to fill you with His Spirit. Then you can know by faith that you are walking in the strength and power of the Lord.

D.L. Moody was one of the greatest evangelists of all time. Huge crowds gathered wherever he spoke. During his lifetime, perhaps a million people gave their lives to Christ as a result of his ministry. D.L. Moody relied on the Holy Spirit for power in ministry. He said, "If a man is filled with the Holy Spirit, then there is no room for the world, then there is no room for self, then there is no room for unholy ambitions and unholy desires, then there is no room for self-seeking and lauding self; but a man will have the mind Christ had when he is filled with the Spirit."[1]

The story is told of a news reporter who attended one of D.L. Moody's evangelistic meetings to find out the secret to the great attraction. He wrote in his news column the next day on Moody: "He butchers the King's English...I see nothing in Mr. Moody to account for his marvelous success." Moody read the article, and when he read that statement, he smiled and said, "That's the secret!" Although I read of that experience with Moody many years ago, I have never forgotten it.

Recently I spoke at a retreat where each woman was given a stone to write out a life-defining phrase that she never wanted to forget. I took my stone and wrote out the words *No Earthly Reason*. I want my life to be defined by my weakness and His strength and sufficiency.

R.A. Torrey, the first superintendant of Moody Bible Institute, tells the story of a man with whom he was closely associated in a great evangelistic movement in the United States. They were having a highly successful convention in Buffalo, and the man was elated. As they walked down the street together to one of the meetings, he remarked to Torrey, "Torrey, you and I are the most important men in Christian work in this country." Torrey replied: "John, I am sorry to hear you say that; for as I read my Bible I find man after man who had accomplished great things whom God had to set aside because of his sense of his own importance." And God did, in fact, set that man aside from that time, and no one heard of him after that experience. R.A. Torrey says, "The entire shore of the history of Christian workers is strewn with the wrecks of gallant vessels that were full of promise a few years ago, but these men became puffed up and were driven on the rocks by the wild winds of their own raging self-esteem." Realize your own inadequacy and rely on His sufficiency.

Great hope is attached to the promises of God in the Bible because every promise takes you beyond your own miniscule resources to the infinite resources of God. That is why your inadequacies become the qualification for experiencing His sufficiencies. Paul said, "Not that we are adequate in ourselves to consider anything as coming from ourselves, but our adequacy is from God" (2 Corinthians 3:5).

Paul suffered what he called "a thorn in the flesh." Commentators are puzzled to this day as to the identity of the thorn. I am glad the thorn is unknown; this way, Paul's statement can apply to all of us. When Paul asked the Lord to take the thorn away, the Lord responded, "My grace is sufficient for you, for power is perfected in weakness." Paul concluded, "Most gladly, therefore, I will rather boast about my weaknesses, so that the power of Christ may dwell in me" (2 Corinthians 12:9).

Martin Luther said, "God creates out of nothing. Therefore, until a man is nothing, God can make nothing of him." John Flavel said, "When God intends to fill a soul, He first makes it empty. When He intends to enrich a soul, He first makes it poor. When He intends to exalt a soul, He first makes it sensible to its own miseries, wants, and nothingness." Richard Halverson said, "The tallest men are those who bend before God." D.L. Moody would often get down on his face before God and ask God to empty him of all self-sufficiency. God answered his prayer.

J.I. Packer paints this picture: "When we walk along a clear road feeling fine, and someone takes our arm to help us, as likely as not we shall impatiently shake him off; but when we are caught in rough country in the dark, with a storm getting up and our strength spent, and someone takes our arm to help us, we shall thankfully lean on him."[2] Mark your calendar the day you realize, *I can't, but He can.* That will be the day when God can do a mighty work in and through you. It's *none* of us, and *all* of Him.

My Response

DATE:

KEY VERSE: "I can do all things through Him who strengthens me" (Philippians 4:13).

FOR FURTHER THOUGHT: How does knowing you can do all things through Christ give you hope today? Where have you been relying on your own strength? Where in your life do you need the strength and power of the Lord?

MY RESPONSE:

Day Twenty-Two

HE BLESSES ME

Blessed be the God and Father of
our Lord Jesus Christ, who has blessed
us with every spiritual blessing in
the heavenly places in Christ.

EPHESIANS 1:3

You are blessed by God with every spiritual blessing. This is one of your crowning glories as His child. Whether you are homeless or you live in a palace, you possess the blessings of God. "Blessed be the God and Father of our Lord Jesus Christ, who has blessed us with every spiritual blessing in the heavenly places in Christ" (Ephesians 1:3). This is an encouraging promise, especially if you face a loss of health, home, finances, or possessions. Oh, what a promise to write from your heavenly checking account, for you will often need the hope it offers.

Have you ever heard someone say, "Yes, God has really blessed me"? People often say that in response to a comment about their many possessions, great job, good health, or abundance of money. And it is true, they are blessed if they know Christ, but not necessarily because of their success or lack of troubles here on earth. In fact, James paints a different picture. He says, "But the brother of humble circumstances is to glory in his high position; and the rich man is to glory in his humiliation, because like flowering grass he will pass away…so too the rich man in the midst of his pursuits will fade away" (James 1:9-11). This simply means that wealth does not define a person's true spiritual blessings. Some very wealthy people do not know the Lord, and they are poor indeed. Others with immense wealth and possessions can boast of an intimate relationship with the Lord, and they are truly rich. I heard Corrie ten Boom share about a man who "sadly, had many riches." Her audience laughed in response to her statement, so she responded, "You laugh, but so often it is not the man who has the money, but the money has the man."

How do you define your blessings? By the things you own? By the money you possess? By your relationships? By good health? Those are indeed blessings as they come to you from God. But you need to know that you are blessed even when you seem to have nothing and trouble comes your way. Many blessings are completely untouchable and can never be taken from you. Because these heavenly blessings are always yours, you can say you are blessed even if you lose your job, you become ill with a life-threatening disease, you lose your house, or you face financial disaster. You have been "blessed with every spiritual blessing in the heavenly places in Christ" (Ephesians 1:3).

What is a blessing? The Greek word *eulogia* refers to the divine favor and benefit of God. We have been given every spiritual benefit. Wuest believes this covers "all the good that comes to us by grace—whether the assurance of immortality, the promise of the resurrection, the inheritance of the kingdom of heaven, the privilege of adoption, etc."[1] The Greek synonym for *eulogia* is *makarios,* which is used in the beatitudes (Blessed are…) and describes one who possesses the favor of God. You are in the world but not of the world. Your satisfaction comes from God and not from favorable circumstances.

Your spiritual blessings are in the heavenly places in Christ. Wuest explains, "It is that we saints while still in the body on earth, are enjoying some of the blessings which we will enjoy in heaven." Heaven will tell the real story of our spiritual wealth. Then you will see exactly how rich you are. Now, we "walk by faith, not by sight" (2 Corinthians 5:7).

What are some of your specific spiritual blessings? They include your position in Christ, holiness, adoption by God as sons and daughters, the glory of His grace, redemption, forgiveness of sin, knowledge of the mystery of His will, an eternal inheritance, and the indwelling Holy Spirit (Ephesians 1:4-14). The fact that you are "in Christ" means you have access to His "glorious, unlimited resources" (Ephesians 3:16 NLT). You are an heir "according to the hope of eternal life" (Titus 3:7) and have an "inheritance which is imperishable and undefiled and will not fade away, reserved in heaven for you" (1 Peter 1:4).

When you realize that you have an inheritance waiting in heaven for you, you discover this world is not your home. Your real citizenship is in heaven, and as author Ruth Paxson says, "Your present address is just a stopping place on a journey" to your real home in heaven. She points out that the biblical phrase "in Christ" implies that we share all things of Christ. "All that Christ possesses we possess. Every spiritual blessing in Him—joy, peace, victory, power, holiness—is ours *here* and *now*. If we are a child of God, then we are His heir and a joint-heir with Christ, so that all the Father has given to His Son, the Son shares with us."[2]

When you realize all the blessings that are yours in Christ, you discover there is absolutely no reason to boast in yourself, and every reason to boast in the Lord! In fact, we know from Paul's words that God has chosen the foolish things of the world and the weak things of the world to "shame the wise" and "shame the things which are strong" (1 Corinthians 1:27). "Let him who boasts, boast in the Lord" (1 Corinthians 1:31). Whether you are "nothing" or "something" in this world, always define who you are and what you have by what you have been given in Christ. Hold everything else with an open hand, knowing it all belongs to the Lord.

Frances Havergal, English poet and hymn writer of the 1800s, became a Christian at the age of 13. She was gifted in music and litera-ture. After reading a little book titled *All for Jesus,* she realized all that was hers in Christ. No longer did she define her life by what she wrote or composed but by the blessings of Christ. She experienced the peace that passes all understanding. This newfound joy and peace was tested almost immediately when her publisher in America went bankrupt in the panic of 1873. She wrote this to a friend,

> I have just had such a blessing in the shape of what would have been only two months ago a really bitter blow to me; and now it is actual accession of joy, because I find that it does not even touch me! Two months ago this would have

been a real trial for me, for I had built a good deal on my American prospects, now *Thy will be done* is not a sigh but only a *song!* I think if it had been all my English footing, present and prospective, as well as the American, that I thus found suddenly gone, it would have been worth it, for the joy it has been to find my Lord so faithful and true to all His promises.[3]

Frances Havergal went on to write many beloved hymns that have blessed those in the church for more than a hundred years, including "I Am Trusting Thee, Lord Jesus," "Like a River Glorious," and "Take My Life and Let It Be."

When you truly realize your gift of "every spiritual blessing in the heavenly places in Christ," you discover a new desire in your heart. In your conversation with the Lord, you will ask, *Lord, what can I do? What can I give You in return?* And while He gives you all freely as a gift of His grace, He will respond and lead you to the kind of commitment found in the words of Frances Havergal:

> Take my life and let it be
> Consecrated, Lord, to Thee.
> Take my hands and let them move
> At the impulse of Thy love,
> At the impulse of Thy love.
>
> Take my love, my God, I pour
> At thy feet its treasure store.
> Take myself and I will be
> Ever, only all for Thee,
> Ever, only all for Thee.

My Response

DATE:

KEY VERSE: "Blessed be the God and Father of our Lord Jesus Christ, who has blessed us with every spiritual blessing in the heavenly places in Christ" (Ephesians 1:3).

FOR FURTHER THOUGHT: What does it mean to you to be blessed with every spiritual blessing? Have you learned to recognize the many different shapes of a blessing? What truth gives you hope from your reading today? What did you learn from the example of Frances Havergal? Have you learned what she learned?

MY RESPONSE:

Day Twenty-Three

HE PRODUCES
FRUIT IN ME

*I am the vine, you are the branches; He who
abides in Me and I in him, he bears much
fruit, for apart from Me you can do nothing.*

JOHN 15:5

When you remain in vital contact with Jesus, your life will be productive and will count for eternity. This is the promise for you in Jesus' words in John 15:5: "I am the vine, you are the branches; he who abides in Me and I in him, he bears much fruit, for apart from Me you can do nothing." The Greek word translated "fruit" is *karpos* and literally refers to produce, but metaphorically it refers to the evidence of life within. When you write the check on this promise, you have the high privilege of enjoying intimacy with your Lord and a life of influence.

Jesus spoke these words during the last week of His life on earth. He knew He would soon be departing this world to go to the Father. He had shared one last meal with His disciples. Then, following the meal, he removed his outer garment, and one by one, washed His disciples' feet. Following this act of love, He began talking with them and teaching them for one last time. This private time was intimate, penetrating, and powerful. Jesus knew His beloved disciples could have no idea of the horror to come. But He knew a time of suffering was imminent and that His own death would deal a devastating blow that would scatter His disciples. They would become frightened and fragmented and lose all hope. What is life all about? What does it all mean? How are we to live?

This is what Jesus addressed in His farewell discourse in John 14–16 and specifically in John 15:5 when He said, "I am the vine, you are the branches; he who abides in Me and I in him, he bears much fruit, for apart from Me you can do nothing." Oh, how we need this vital promise just as much as the disciples did. Like them, we have days of disillusionment and discouragement and wonder how we are going to endure.

In John 15:5 the Master Teacher uses the picture of a vine and branches to illustrate your dynamic relationship with Him. In this picture, He is showing you, first of all, that He is the true source of life. The branches have no life apart from the vine. They draw everything they need to grow from the vine. And so it is with you. Your life comes from Jesus. So often, in the heat of a trial, we will run to outside sources for meaning and purpose in life. Always remember the promise that your life is in Jesus, the true vine.

Then Jesus uses the picture of the vine to show you that an intimate relationship with Him is the true explanation of life. The vine and the branches share an intimate relationship. That is the kind of relationship Jesus desires with you: intimate and personal. This intimacy is seen in the branches' union and communion with the vine and their dependence on it. In the same way, you are united with Christ—your oneness with Him is such that Jesus lives in you and expresses Himself in and through you to touch a lost and hurting world. Your communion with Him is a dynamic fellowship as you interact with Him through prayer and meditation on His Word. You depend and rely on Him as your resource for your highest and deepest longings in your spiritual life.

The picture of the vine and the branches also gives you the true focus in life. Notice this illustration teaches that life is all about the vine. Jesus is your focus, and all of life revolves around Him. He is your eternal

Partner in life and the One who will never leave or forsake you. He is the One worth living for and dying for.

What is the secret to experiencing the intimate relationship with Jesus pictured by the vine and the branches? Very simply, abide in Christ. The Greek word for "abide" is *meno* and means to remain in vital contact. We need these words from Jesus because our hearts are prone to wander, especially in the heat of the battle of life. You enjoy and experience the benefits of intimacy with the Lord only as you remain in vital contact with Him. You maintain this close communion with your Lord by developing a daily quiet time alone with Him. Learn to set aside a time with your Lord each day. Schedule it on your calendar. Establish a place where you will sit alone with Him. Organize all your quiet time materials there. Have a plan to read your Bible, talk with the Lord, and meditate on what you have learned from Him.

Your quiet time with the Lord is the most important part of the day because it enables you to remain in vital contact with the Lord Jesus. I like to use the P.R.A.Y.E.R. Quiet Time Plan:

Prepare Your Heart

Read and Study God's Word

Adore God in Prayer

Yield Yourself to God

Enjoy His Presence

Rest in His Love

You can learn more about this plan by reading *Six Secrets to a Powerful Quiet Time* and by experiencing the books of quiet times in the Quiet Times for the Heart series from Quiet Time Ministries. Imagine how different you will be as you face each day after having spent time with your Lord. Your dependence on Him will be stronger, and you will be more aware of the resources He gives you to face whatever comes your way.

What will be the result of abiding in the vine? Jesus gives you the answer: You will bear much fruit. And something is very significant about this kind of fruit—it remains (John 15:16). In fact, producing fruit that remains is one of the Lord's purposes in you. He says, "You did not choose Me but I chose you, and appointed you that you would go and bear fruit, and that your fruit would remain" (John 15:16). Fruit that remains is fruit that lasts forever. This fruit includes a Christlike character (Galatians 5:22-23), those who come to know Christ as a result of your life with Him (Romans 1:13), and a life lived in a manner worthy of the Lord (Colossians 1:10). This kind of fruit glorifies God (Matthew 5:16), is borne for God and not for ourselves (Romans 7:4), and is possible even during a difficult time (such as a year of drought as we see in Jeremiah 17:7-8). When your life produces fruit that remains, your life counts for eternity. Oh, how we need men and women in this generation who will remain in vital contact with Jesus and live lives that make a difference for all of eternity. These are the people who are willing to set aside the playthings of this world and live for the audience of One, the Lord Jesus Christ.

Audrey Wetherell Johnson grew up in a Christian home. She was a brilliant thinker and went to France for her college education. Under the influence of French intellectuals and secular philosophical studies, her belief in basic biblical truths eroded. By the time she returned home to England, she considered herself an agnostic. Outwardly she seemed to enjoy being home, but her inner life was one of quiet despair. In her search for truth and answers, one night she came across the words of Jesus: "And whosoever liveth and believeth in me shall never die. Believest thou this?" (John 11:26 KJV). When she read those words, she felt as if Jesus were looking into her eyes and speaking directly to her. In an instant she saw that Jesus was the truth, and she gave her life to Him.

Then the adventure began. One thing took precedence over everything else—the Word of God. She loved the Bible. It was the authority for her belief; she believed that God's Word had the supreme right to command her beliefs and actions. She developed a great love and passion for teaching the Word of God.

The Lord led her to become a missionary in China. When Japan invaded China during World War II, she was taken prisoner, something she had dreaded more than anything else. She was finally released, and after some time, she came to the United States, resting and recovering in San Bernardino, California. There she was asked to teach the Bible to five women. Troubled by what she observed as "spoon-feeding" believers the Bible, she developed a study where women went to the Bible firsthand

and studied it for themselves. She wrote out some study questions to help them learn, and she gave them a summary and teaching at the end of each session. These simple sessions with these five women began what became her life's work for the next 20 years—Bible Study Fellowship.

Audrey Wetherell Johnson exemplifies what can happen when a person remains in vital contact with Jesus Christ. The fruit of her life goes well beyond what she ever could have imagined. Only heaven will tell the true story. And so it is with you. Only heaven will tell the story of what will happen when you draw near to the Lord, remain in vital contact with Him, and begin writing checks on His promises. As the man said to D.L. Moody so many years ago: "The world has yet to see what God will do with and for and through and in and by the man who is fully and wholly consecrated to Him." May you and I answer that call.

My Response

DATE:

KEY VERSE: "I am the vine, you are the branches; he who abides in Me and I in him, he bears much fruit, for apart from Me you can do nothing" (John 15:5).

FOR FURTHER THOUGHT: What will it take for you to remain in vital contact with the Lord Jesus? What would you like to be the result of your life here on earth? What will be your legacy? What have you learned today that challenges you and encourages you?

MY RESPONSE:

Day Twenty-Four

QUIET TIME
WEEK FOUR:
HOPE IN
WHAT JESUS
HAS DONE

But may it be that I would never boast,
except in the cross of our Lord Jesus Christ.

GALATIANS 6:14

PREPARE YOUR HEART

Standing tall on the horizon of all of history and reaching from earth to heaven is the cross of Jesus Christ. The cross is central to your life. That is why Paul said, "But may it never be that I would boast, except in the cross of our Lord Jesus Christ" (Galatians 6:14). Why is the cross such a powerful symbol? It represents the greatest work ever accomplished. On the cross, Jesus visibly demonstrated to us that He is indeed our "dread champion" (Jeremiah 20:11). Today you are going to take some time to think about the work of Jesus on the cross. The more you realize it, the more you will have the kind of hope that causes you to stand with your head held high regardless of the storms that come your way. Ask the Lord to open your eyes that you may see wonderful and amazing things in His Word (Psalm 119:18).

READ AND STUDY GOD'S WORD

1. So much is wrapped up in the cross of Jesus Christ. Read Romans 5:6-11 in the Phillips translation:

> And we can see that while we were powerless to help ourselves that Christ died for sinful men. In human experience it is a rare thing for one man to give his life for another, even if the latter be a good man, though there have been a few who have had the courage to do it. Yet the proof of God's amazing love is this: that it was while we were sinners that Christ died for us. Moreover, if he did that for us while we were sinners, now that we are men justified by the shedding of his blood, what reason have we to fear the wrath of God? If, while we were his enemies, Christ reconciled us to God by dying for us, surely now that we are reconciled we may be perfectly certain of our salvation through his living in us. Nor, I am sure, is this a matter of bare salvation—we may hold our heads high in the light of God's love because of the reconciliation which Christ has made.

2. According to Romans 5:6-11, what has the Lord accomplished for you on the cross?

3. Read the following verses and record what you learn about the cross of Christ:

1 Corinthians 1:18

Philippians 2:5-11

Colossians 1:13-14

Hebrews 12:2

1 Peter 2:23-24

ADORE GOD IN PRAYER

Father, I have lost the feeling of Thy presence. Yet deep in my heart I know that it is not because Thou didst leave me, but because I have wandered from Thee.

All we like sheep have gone astray. We have turned every one to his own way. I confess that I have found that way hard and wearisome. My feet are tired of wandering. My heart is sick of being lost. I would return to Thee now and be led of Thee in Thy way, that I may walk once more with a sense of direction and a clear light upon my path.

O my Father, receive me—Thy prodigal child; prodigal because I have wandered in a far country, prodigal in my forgetfulness of Thee, prodigal in all the blessings I have taken for granted. Now, bowing before Thee, I acknowledge them all.

And now I arise and come back to Thee, my Father, knowing that Thou art even now running to meet me, placing over my shoulders the robe of Thy love, placing upon my hand the ring of Thy forgiveness, pressing upon me the kiss of a divine love that knows no limit—a love which loved me while I was yet a sinner—a love that brought Jesus to Calvary.

I thank Thee for that love; I thank Thee for this restoration. I thank Thee that Thou art still my Father, that I am still Thy child. Amen.[1]

PETER MARSHALL

YIELD YOURSELF TO GOD

The cross, then, is the place where God's justice and love meet. God retains the integrity of his justice; God pours out the fullness of his love. In the cross, God shows himself to be just and the one who justifies sinners whose faith rests in his Son. The death of God's own Son is the only adequate gauge of what God thinks of my sin; the death of God's own Son is the only basis on which I may be forgiven that sin. The cross is the triumph of justice and love.[2]

D.A. CARSON

Meditate on these words written by Isaac Watts:

> When I survey the wondrous cross
> On which the Prince of glory died,
> My richest gain I count but loss,
> And pour contempt on all my pride.
>
> Forbid it, Lord, that I should boast,
> Save in the death of Christ my God;
> All the vain things that charm me most,
> I sacrifice them to His blood.
>
> See, from His head, His hands, His feet,
> Sorrow and love flow mingled down;
> Did e'er such love and sorrow meet,
> Or thorns compose so rich a crown?
>
> Were the whole realm of nature mine,
> That were a present far too small;
> Love so amazing, so divine,
> Demands my soul, my life, my all.

ENJOY HIS PRESENCE

What does the cross of Jesus Christ mean to you today? Close your quiet time with those thoughts and write your insights in the space provided.

REST IN HIS LOVE

"We may hold our heads high in the light of God's love because of the reconciliation which Christ has made" (Romans 5:11 PHILLIPS).

Notes — Week Four

Week Five

HOPE IN
WHAT HE SAYS

Days 25–30

Day Twenty-Five

THE WORD OF GOD
LASTS FOREVER

*The grass withers, the flower fades, But
the word of our God stands forever.*

ISAIAH 40:8

You can bank your life on what God says in His Word. Why? Because what God says in the Bible lasts forever. Isaiah summarizes this truth, contrasting the living word of God and the creation: "The grass withers, the flower fades, but the word of our God stands forever" (Isaiah 40:8). Jesus amplifies this truth: "Heaven and earth will pass away, but my words will not pass away" (Matthew 24:35). When all else fails, God and His Word remain steadfast. And in a world that is constantly changing, we can have a great comfort and a great hope that God and His Word never change. In essence, the Bible provides an eternal foundation for your life.

What will be the foundation of your life? Will your life be built on things that last forever or things that will fade away? This decision will determine the course and outcome of your life. This is a focused decision and carries eternal consequences.

Jesus delivered a monumental discourse while on earth—the Sermon on the Mount. In most sermons, the final thoughts are the most important. They are the words that the speaker most earnestly wants the people to remember. Jesus chose to conclude His sermon with powerful truths about His words.

> Everyone who hears these words of Mine and acts on them, may be compared to a wise man who built his house on the rock. And the rain fell, and the floods came, and the winds blew and slammed against that house; and yet it did not fall, for it had been founded on the rock. Everyone who hears these words of Mine and does not act on them, will be like a foolish man who built his house on the sand. The rain fell, and the floods came, and the winds blew and slammed against that house; and it fell—and great was its fall (Matthew 7:24-27).

These words are teaching you the great value of finding hope in the promises of God. When you find the promise, embrace the promise, trust the promise, and live the promise, you are like the wise man who built his house on the rock. You have made the best choice. That is why you can have hope—**H**olding **O**n with **P**atient **E**xpectation. Regardless of how great the flood or powerful the wind, your foundation cannot be shaken because it is built on the sound rock of the Word of God. Life does, indeed, come down to this one decision. What are you using to build the house of your life? Are you using the Word of God or the things of the world as your building material? You can never go wrong with the Word of God.

The Bible, the Word of God, lasts forever (Isaiah 40:8). The words, opinions, and feelings of men are as unreliable and ever-changing as the weather. The Word of God, on the other hand, rests on the character of the eternal God, the Creator of the universe. In uncertain days of looking for a job many years ago, I relied on the promise of God in Jeremiah 29:11: "'I know the plans that I have for you,' declares the LORD, 'plans for welfare and not for calamity to give you a future and a hope.'" Not long after I claimed this promise, the Lord did indeed provide a job for me that led to an effective ministry where dozens came to know Him.

The Bible, the Word of God, is living and active and able to judge the thoughts and intentions of the heart (Hebrews 4:12). According to 1 Samuel 16:7, we know that "God sees not as man sees, for man looks at the outward appearance, but the LORD looks at the heart." Because God sees your heart, what He says is directed to your heart and effects a transformation and change in your life. During a particularly stressful period of my life, when I read Genesis 8:1, "But God remembered Noah," I did not realize my own level of despair. The Lord, who knows my heart better than I know it, saw my sadness and used His Word to lift me up. As a result, the house of my life became stronger as I rested my hope on His promise to pay special attention to me and lavish His love and care and concern in my life.

The Bible, the Word of God, is inspired by God, is profitable for teaching, for reproof, for correction, for training in righteousness, and makes you adequate and equipped for every good work (2 Timothy 3:16-17). Your teacher and your place of study will determine the quality of your character and the standard of your work. Men and women who want to become physicians choose their medical schools, internships, and residencies very carefully, knowing these things will determine their own standard of excellence and future quality of care for their patients. In the same way, you can know that the Bible will give you everything you need to face the trials and triumphs in life. It is written by God Himself, your Master Teacher, who designed you for His glory.

Many years ago, I made a decision to know what God says in His Word better than I know anything else. I bought books that taught me how to study the Bible. I attended in-depth Bible studies that used the Word of God as the textbook. I refused to settle for less than learning what God had to say to me about every area of my life. As a result, I have confidence that His Word is always relevant for me. When I have a question about life, I first consult what God says in His Word, not what man says in the world. The words of men can lead to fear, but the Word of God leads to faith. "Faith comes from hearing, and hearing by the word of Christ" (Romans 10:17). No wonder God encourages us to be extravagant with the Word (Colossians 3:16) and to study it (2 Timothy 2:15). We never waste time when we spend it in the Bible.

Samuel Rutherford said, "There is but a certain quality of spiritual force in any one man. Spread it over a broad surface, the stream is shallow and languid; narrow the channel and it becomes a driving force." If you only sample the Bible and play with it, you will be shallow. But if you will go deep in the Word of God, you will become a driving force in the kingdom of God by the power of the Holy Spirit. R.A. Torrey asserts that "ninety-nine Christians in every hundred are merely playing at Bible study; and therefore ninety-nine Christians in every hundred are mere weaklings, when they might be giants, both in their Christian life and in their service." If you know you need to stop being a spiritual weakling and start studying like a spiritual giant, become intentional! Write the check on the promise and resolve to build your life on the eternal foundation of the Word of God. Oh, that we might have a whole generation of spiritual giants!

My Response

DATE:

KEY VERSE: "The grass withers, the flower fades, but the word of our God stands forever" (Isaiah 40:8).

FOR FURTHER THOUGHT: Have you made the decision to build your life on the foundation of the eternal Word of God? How do you think building your life on what God says in His Word will make a difference in a person's life? What must we do with the Word of God in order for it to be our foundation in life?

MY RESPONSE:

Day Twenty-Six

YOUR TIMES ARE IN HIS HAND

But as for me, I trust in You, O
LORD, I say, "You are my God."
My times are in Your hand.

PSALM 31:14-15

God holds the events of your life in His hand. When you wonder what is going on in your life and when you feel as though life is passing you by, get out your spiritual pen and write a check on this promise. David, the man after God's own heart, said to the Lord in the midst of his own affliction, "My times are in Your hand" (Psalm 31:15). The Hebrew word for "times" is *et* and covers a broad spectrum from simple occasions and circumstances to vast opportunities and seasons of your life. What a comfort for you in your trials, afflictions, stresses, storms, and suffering.

Early on in my relationship with the Lord I read two powerful books written by Joni Eareckson Tada: *Joni* and *A Step Further*. As a teenager, she had invited Christ into her life at a summer Young Life Camp. But on July 30, 1967, she dove into shallow water of the Chesapeake Bay,

193

and in a moment that changed her life, she was paralyzed from the neck down. After many weeks of intensive therapy for her neck injury, she began rehabilitation and physical therapy at a nursing home, battling self-pity and depression—a severe testing of her faith. Friends read her the Bible, *Mere Christianity* by C.S Lewis, and works by Francis Schaeffer. One of her occupational therapists recommended that she try drawing using an artist's pen in her mouth. A talented artist prior to her accident, she was soon producing amazing works of art. Through a series of doors that God opened for her, she began receiving invitations to speak at area churches. The turning point for her ministry came when she appeared on Barbara Walter's *Today Show* in New York and shared her story with millions of people. As a result, her worldwide ministry, Joni and Friends, was born.

What lifted Joni from being merely a paralytic to being an effective minister for the Lord? Her wheelchair became a pulpit instead of a prison. She had immersed herself in God's Word and focused on claiming His promises. When Larry King on CNN television asked her how she kept such a joyful attitude, she related this insight about her situation: When she is lying in her bed and hears her friend who has come to her home to help her with her morning routine, she often does not feel like getting up or being cheerful. Wanting to have a grateful, cheerful heart, she prays a prayer: *Jesus, I don't have a smile today, so can I borrow one of yours?* And perhaps she remembers the words of the psalmist, "Why are you down in the dumps, dear soul? Why are you crying the blues? Fix my eyes on God—soon I'll be praising again. He puts a smile on my face. He's my God" (Psalm 42:5 MSG).

Joni speaks of her suffering this way: "In the Psalms we're told that God does not deal with us according to our sins and iniquities. My accident was not a punishment for my wrongdoing—whether or not I deserved it. Only God knows why I was paralyzed." Joni Eareckson, one of my heroes of the faith, taught me that God can take the seemingly worst tragedy and use it for His glory. Joni is a testimony of the powerful life of God in the soul of man. The explanation for the smile on her face and the life she lives is the power and presence of the Lord Jesus Christ.

You may be thinking, *Yes, but you don't know my situation. I didn't ask for this trial, I don't want it, and I don't know why it's happening. I'm experiencing tragedy and trauma of the utmost degree.* Amy Carmichael, who experienced a tragic accident that left her crippled, said, "It is not wrong, nor does God condemn us for wishing it need never be."[1] But you need to know that tragedy can become triumph because you are in God's hand. Even if you do not know the whys and hows of trauma, tragedy, and suffering, you can find comfort in the mighty hand that is holding you and guiding the course of your life. Knowing you are in His hand takes you beyond the crush of despair to the victory of hope. His hand holds our birth, our death, our life, our length of days, our successes and failures, our relationships (good and bad), our tears and sorrows, our joys and expectations, and yes, even our prayers. Life seems impossible at times, but God's hand lifts you up.

In the Lord's hand, your greatest disappointments can become His appointments. His broad hand is creatively at work in and through you. His hand can restore lost years (Joel 2:25), cause all things to work together for good (Romans 8:28), give you all good things (Psalm 84:11), refresh you (Acts 3:19), and manifest through you the sweet aroma of the knowledge of Him in every place (2 Corinthians 2:14). His hand made you His workmanship created in Christ Jesus for a purpose—to do good works that He prepared beforehand (Ephesians 2:10). Jesus is with you, for we know that He is at the right hand of God (Mark 16:19; Romans 8:34). God's hand will exalt you at exactly the proper time and will perfect, confirm, strengthen, and establish you (1 Peter 5:6,10). Take comfort in the hand that holds you. It is the large and powerful hand of God.

No wonder Psalm 31 came into Jesus' mind in the moments before He died on the cross, when He cried out, "Into Your hand I commit my spirit" (Psalm 31:5). This is the great cry of one who trusts the promise that "my times are in Your hand" (Psalm 31:15). And surely no one suffered a more cruel, inhumane, undeserved treatment than Jesus on the cross. And yet we know the explanation for His suffering, the *why* of His death on the cross—He was sacrificing Himself on our behalf, paying the price for our sin (Isaiah 53; John 3:16). We also know He sympathizes with our weakness, for He knows the depths of our suffering (Hebrews 4:15) as the man of sorrows (Isaiah 53:3). And He is our example—in His suffering, He was able to commit His spirit to the Father.

God did not give Job a reason for his suffering. D.A. Carson points out that "Job teaches us that, at least in this world, there will always remain some mysteries to suffering. He also teaches us to exercise faith—not blind, thoughtless submission to an impersonal status quo, but faith in the God who has graciously revealed himself to us."[2] God revealed Himself to Job in an incredibly intimate and uniquely powerful way. Job's response to God was, "I know that You can do all things, and that no purpose of Yours can be thwarted...I have heard of You by the hearing of the ear; but now my eye sees You; therefore I retract, and I repent in dust and ashes" (Job 42:1-6). Then Job prayed for his friends. The Lord eventually restored to Job all his possessions and increased all that he had twofold (Job 42:10). We learn from Job that certain events of our lives are incomprehensible because we are not God. Amy Carmichael, who knew the dark side of suffering, said, "Perhaps if we could shut our eyes on the world's way of looking at things, and go to sleep with our head on a stone, we should see all the obstructing, all the impossible, changed as it were to a ladder beside us, set on the earth, the top reaching to heaven."[3]

We do walk by faith and not by sight (2 Corinthians 5:7). Paul encourages us to "fight the good fight of faith. Take hold of the eternal life to which you were called" (1 Timothy 6:12). Trusting that our times are in His hands is indeed a fight because the promise is so opposite of our feelings. And we know that we will experience more of the "good fight of faith" in the future—and the battles will not be easy and will often be difficult to comprehend.

After Corrie ten Boom's stroke, she received the most discouraging news of all from her therapists—she would probably never speak again. They had hoped that speech therapy might help her, but the results of the tests were discouraging. According to her assistant's memoirs, Corrie showed no signs of disappointment on the way home from the medical appointment, or even that night while they watched television. But later that evening, Pamela, her assistant, brought milk and cookies to Corrie and witnessed something she had never seen before—Corrie was weeping openly. Corrie's childlike trust had not wavered, but she surely felt the pain of living in an earthly body that was withering away. Pamela describes a morning near the end of Corrie's life when she sat and held

Corrie's hand as they looked out the window at some beautiful birds. Pamela describes how she turned back toward Corrie and saw that she was not looking at the birds but at Pamela and her eyes were full of love. Pamela said, "As I received that look, I too became full of love. And I marveled again at the communication that is possible in silence."[4] Corrie ten Boom went home to be with the Lord on her ninety-first birthday. Her life is an example of one whose times were truly in the hand of the Lord. She embraced, trusted, and lived the promise of Psalm 31:15.

The same hand that holds you now is also going to one day wipe every tear from your eyes, take away death, take away mourning, take away crying, and take away pain forever. These tragedies, the result of a fallen, temporal world, will pass away and make way for a new heaven and a new earth that are eternal (Revelation 21:1-4). Praise the Lord that the hand of the Lord makes all things new—the ultimate triumph over tragedy.

> And He who sits on the throne said, "Behold I am making all things new." And He said, "Write, for these words are faithful and true" (Revelation 21:5).

My Response

DATE:

KEY VERSE: "My times are in Your hand" (Psalm 31:15).

FOR FURTHER THOUGHT: How does knowing that your times are in His hand bring hope and comfort to you? What does it mean to you? What do you need from the Lord today? Will you bring your burdens to the One who holds you in His hand?

MY RESPONSE:

THE AUDIENCE OF ONE

Therefore, my beloved brethren, be steadfast, immovable, always abounding in the work of the Lord, knowing that your toil is not in vain in the Lord.

1 CORINTHIANS 15:58

Your ministry is measured by faithfulness, not fame and fortune. Paul said, "Therefore, my beloved brethren, be steadfast, immovable, always abounding in the work of the Lord, knowing that your toil is not in vain in the Lord" (1 Corinthians 15:58). I love this promise. It was the first verse I ever memorized after I gave my life to the Lord. I have been thinking about these words for a long, long time. This is the promise for you to count on when you are in the trenches, laboring in the ministry God has entrusted to you. Your success in ministry is determined by God, not man, and is measured by how you live your life before the audience of one. "When God is our audience, our best acts are often a beautiful secret between Him and us."[1] In this verse, God gives you three exhortations and a promise to help you carry out His will for your life.

The first exhortation is to be steadfast. The Greek word translated "steadfast" is *hedraios* and means to be steady and settled in your mind and purpose. Other translations and paraphrases use the following words for "steadfast": "stand your ground" (MSG), "be firm" (AMP), "be strong" (NLT), and "stand firm" (NIV). In the context of 1 Corinthians 15:58, Paul is encouraging the Corinthians to be strong and stand their ground with their goal and purpose clearly in mind.

Being clear about your goal in life is imperative if you would continue on your course of ministry without giving up. A thousand and one obstacles, large and small, will stand in your way. Being steadfast in your goal will keep you running your race when the labor becomes difficult. Paul's goal ordered his direction and decisions in life. Paul said, "I do all things for the sake of the gospel" (1 Corinthians 9:23). My personal and ministry goal is to know God intimately and to make Him known to others. I am clear about wanting others to experience an intimate relationship with the Lord. I measure every opportunity that comes my way against my goal.

Next, we are exhorted to be immovable. "Immovable" is a translation of the Greek word *ametakinetos* and means firm and secure. You are to "let nothing move you" in ministry (Phillips). "Don't be shaken" (CEV) when you are in the trenches and are laboring to the point of exhaustion in what God has called you to accomplish. Threats may come your way, either real or imagined. You may receive harsh criticism. You may suffer a financial difficulty. The encouragement here is to stand firm in the Lord.

And then Paul exhorts us to be people who are "always abounding in the work of the Lord." To "abound" is a translation of *perisseuo* and means to go above and beyond; it is a superlative command to give more than enough, more than the task requires. In essence, you are to go above and beyond in every assignment the Lord gives to you. The Amplified Bible puts it this way:

> Therefore, my beloved brethren, be firm (steadfast), immovable, always abounding in the work of the Lord (always being superior, excelling, doing more than enough in the service of the Lord), knowing and being continually aware that your labor in the Lord is not futile (it is never wasted or to no purpose).

Finally, Paul motivates us to carry out these strong exhortations with a reminder that our "toil is not in vain in the Lord." *Kopos,* the Greek word for "toil," refers to the weariness that accompanies exhausting physical or mental exertion. Your weariness in ministry should never cause you to stop running your race. Why? Because you know that what you do is never useless or wasted when you do it before the audience of one. Living for the audience of one means you carry out your ministry "in the Lord." David says, "Surely the godly are praising your name, for they will live in your presence" (Psalm 140:13 NLT). Living for the audience of one means that everything we do is done in the presence of the Lord Jesus. Jesus taught this principle when He said, "I tell you the truth, whatever you did for one of the least of these brothers of mine, you did for me" (Matthew 25:40 NIV). Imagine that we are living on a stage, but the performance hall has only one seat in the audience, and Jesus is sitting in that seat. If we are running a race, He is the only Person in the crowd. If we are writing a paper, we will turn it in to Jesus alone—He alone will give us the ultimate grade. If we are washing the dishes in our home, Jesus is in the kitchen woth us. A.W. Tozer summarizes this focus on Christ:

> If you are living only to buy and sell and get gain, that is not enough. If you are living only to sleep and work, that is not enough. If you are living only to prosper and marry and raise a family, that is not enough. If you live only to get old and die, and never find forgiveness and the daily sense of God's presence in your life, you have missed God's great purpose for you...Build that invisible altar within. Let the Spirit of God produce the living, cleansing flame that marks your devotion to Christ, our Lord.[2]

Twenty-year-old Jim Elliot prayed, "Lord, make my way prosperous, not that I may achieve high station, but that my life may be an exhibit to the value of knowing God."[3] The sweet aroma of His life in you, as you walk with Him, is delivering the knowledge of Him to others everywhere you go and in whatever you do. Whether you are discipling your children, working in an office answering phones and filing papers, living alone in assisted living, leading a Bible study, cooking a meal for your family, suffering in a hospital bed, slaving at a computer, or conducting strategic board meetings for a major corporation, God is doing a mighty work in and through you as you live for an audience of one and run your race for Him. You may not see it now, but eternity will tell the story of your faithfulness to live for an audience of one.

According to Paul in 1 Corinthians 12:4-6, God gives varieties of "gifts...ministries...and effects," but "the same God who works all things in all persons." Ultimately, the Lord is doing all the work. I like to think of ministry as Jesus Christ in action because He works in and through us. All ministry is a stewardship the Lord has entrusted to us. Paul said, "Of this church I was made a minister according to the stewardship from God bestowed on me for your benefit, so that I might fully carry out the preaching of the word of God" (Colossians 1:25). "Stewardship" is a translation of the Greek word *oikonomia* and implies a responsibility entrusted to you from the Lord. Those responsibilities result in ministry, and the Lord uses them to produce the results He desires. Your mission is to give your best to the audience of one, your Lord Jesus Christ, and then to leave the results with Him. As Ney Bailey, author and speaker for Campus Crusade for Christ, told me many years ago, "You be responsible for the depth of your ministry, and let God be responsible for the breadth of your ministry."

I learned this principle of ministry early in my relationship with Christ as the Lord gave me outstanding examples to emulate. The writer of Hebrews exhorts us to "remember those who led you, who spoke the word of God to you; and considering the result of their conduct, imitate their faith" (Hebrews 13:7). I think of my mother, the most faithful woman of God I have ever known. Perhaps the greatest example for me in ministry was Josh McDowell, a servant of the Lord with all his heart and soul. I watched him labor hard in ministry every waking hour of the day. Whether he was writing, speaking, or ministering on a college campus, he remained focused on the service at hand, never on popularity or promotion of himself. I am thankful for these examples because they helped me understand the great value of faithfulness in ministry. I learned to run my race for the Lord, not for man.

I learned the most about living for the audience of one while I attended seminary. Examinations and grades commanded our focus to a great extent. I realized that writing papers and reading books were labors that the Lord Jesus was giving me to do for Him. He was training me for His purposes. As a result, I gave each assignment my very best. And I carry that same perspective with me as I continue to run the race set before me. The dance of life for the audience of one looks for the greatest reward of all—the words "well done good and faithful servant" (Matthew 25:21 NIV).

That "your labor is not in vain in the Lord" is the promise for anyone who has a heart for ministry. Write the check on this promise. Holding On with Patient Expectation will encourage you to carry out your ministry with excellence even if it is for one person. Paul says, "Whatever you do, do your work heartily, as for the Lord rather than for men" (Colossians 3:23). Jim Elliot concluded that a person must "live to the hilt every situation you believe to be the will of God."[4] This, I believe, is what God honors in ministry. Nothing we do is simply putting in time until we achieve success and receive accolades. What we are doing now, faithful in the moment, for the audience of one, is the ultimate success in ministry. It happens on the job, in our home, at our church, and everywhere out in the world.

I remember a speaking engagement out in the middle of the desert in Yucca Valley, California, a place so obscure that the directions instructed us to "turn left at the white rock." When Cindy, my traveling assistant, and I read that, we laughed—we loved it! The luncheon was attended by about 50 women from a number of churches in the area. I thought, *Lord, why did You bring me out here in the middle of nowhere?* When I finished my message, I gave an invitation to receive Christ. After we left, on the way home, we looked at all the response cards. A woman had prayed and invited Jesus to come into her life. I cried because that speaking engagement showed me so much about the heart of the Lord. He will go to the ends of the earth to save one soul. And if He wants to do it through me, who am I to say no? We must say, *Yes Lord—wherever and whenever.* We must always live, not for the audience of the world, but for the audience of one.

My Response

DATE:

KEY VERSE: "Therefore, my beloved brethren, be steadfast, immovable, always abounding in the work of the Lord, knowing that your toil is not in vain in the Lord" (1 Corinthians 15:58).

FOR FURTHER THOUGHT: Who have been your examples in ministry, and what has been the greatest lesson you've learned? What does it mean to live for the audience of one? What ministry has the Lord entrusted to you? How will what you have read today encourage you in ministry?

MY RESPONSE:

Day Twenty-Eight

A PLACE FOR YOU

*Do not let your heart be troubled;
believe in God, believe also in Me. In My
Father's house are many dwelling places;
if it were not so, I would have told you;
for I go to prepare a place for you. If I go
and prepare a place for you, I will come
again and receive you to Myself, that
where I am, there you may be also.*

JOHN 14:1-3

Your real home is in heaven; this world, with all its glitter and glamour, is not your home. Never sink your roots down too deeply in this world, for you are a pilgrim of the Lord on a pilgrimage of the heart. Jesus, even now, is preparing a place for you. That's His promise. Someday He will come and bring you to that place where He is. He says, "In my Father's house are many dwelling places; if it were not so, I would have told you; for I go to prepare a place for you. If I go and prepare a place for you, I will come again and receive you to Myself, that where I am, there you may be also" (John 14:2-3). Write the check on this promise when you are feeling that life is at an end, that life has lost its meaning, and that you do not think you have anything to look forward to in the future.

Nothing can touch your heavenly home. Jesus says, "Do not lay up for yourselves treasures on earth, where moth and rust destroy and where thieves break in and steal, but lay up for yourselves treasures in heaven, where neither moth nor rust destroys, and where thieves do not break in and steal. For where your treasure is, there will your heart be also" (Matthew 6:19-21). We are traveling in a foreign land, and one day we will reach our real residence, where we have our true citizenship. The heroes of the faith in Hebrews 11 are those who "confessed that they were strangers and exiles on the earth. For those who say such things make it clear that they are seeking a country of their own...they desire a better country, that is, a heavenly one. Therefore God is not ashamed to be called their God; for He has prepared a city for them" (Hebrews 11:13-16). Paul reminded the suffering church at Philippi that "our citizenship is in heaven, from which also we eagerly wait for a Savior, the Lord Jesus Christ; who will transform the body of our humble state into conformity with the body of His glory, by the exertion of the power that He has even to subject all things to Himself" (Philippians 3:20-21). These powerful promises clearly show that this life, though palpable and real to us in the present, is neither all there is now nor even the best there is for our future.

A number of years ago, my husband and I sold what I had always considered to be my permanent home. It was almost perfect in every way. I even had my own study with most of my books immediately at hand. The study even had an incredible view. One day, I was looking out the window with tears in my eyes, trying to come to grips with what was, to me, a huge loss. But then I turned to the promises of God related to eternity and my eternal home. I thought, *John 14:1-2 promises that God has prepared a place for me in heaven, Matthew 6:19 promises that my treasure is in heaven, and Philippians 3:20-21 promises that my citizenship is in heaven.* I thought, *Okay that settles it—I am going to have to leave this house someday because the Lord is going to take me home to be with Him. This house is not going with me. And even if I live in this house all my days on earth, I am going to have to say goodbye to it when I die. So why not say goodbye to it now and go on to something new the Lord has planned for me? It really doesn't matter where I live on earth because I am never really home until I am with the Lord face-to-face.* The Lord had shown me a great truth that would have been obvious to most people but was not immediately apparent to me. My reasoning with the Lord and His promises set me free to let my favorite house go. I no longer look at the house where I live as home—my home, my dwelling place, is with the Lord, and I am not truly home until I meet Him face-to-face in heaven.

What is our home in heaven going to be like? Heaven is a new city, the New Jerusalem described in Revelation 21–22. It is a new place for us with a new appearance of glory and holiness, where we feel completely at home. My mother, who recently sold her dream house and moved into assisted living, believes the Lord is preparing her for her heavenly home. Living where she is now has caused her to realize that the place Jesus prepares for us is where we will really live—it is home. Heaven will give us a new life designed by God—a life of service, satisfaction, and fellowship with each other and with God Himself (Revelation 22). In heaven we are going to experience a new relationship with the triune God (Revelation 21:3). We will see His face (Revelation 22:4)! Our faith will become sight. We will enjoy intimacy and fellowship with our God as they were always meant to be. We will experience eternal companionship with our Lord Jesus Christ. What a joy to be face-to-face with Him!

Spurgeon tells the story of two brothers. One had been attentive to and successful in his worldly business but neglected "true religion." The other brother was diligent in serving Christ, distributed his goods to the poor, and for the sake of his conscience, sacrificed many opportunities of gain. When the devout brother lay sick and dying in difficult circumstances, his wealthy brother reproved him, remarking that if not for his religion, he would not be dependent on others for financial help. With great calm, the saintly brother replied, "O Tom, I have a kingdom and an inheritance I have not yet seen."

Charles Fuller (1887–1968), a preacher and director of *The Old-Fashioned Revival Hour* radio program, announced that he was going to be speaking the next week on heaven. During that week of preparation, he received a letter from an older man who was very ill:

> Next Sunday you are to talk about heaven. I am interested in that land, because I have held a clear title to a bit of property there for over 55 years. I did not buy it. It was given to me without money and without price. But the

Donor purchased it for me at tremendous sacrifice. I am not holding it for speculation since it is not transferable. It is not a vacant lot. For more than half a century I have been sending materials out of which the greatest Architect and Builder of the universe has been building a home for me which will never need to be remodeled or repaired because it will suit me perfectly, individually, and will never grow old. Termites can never undermine its foundations for they rest on the rock of ages. Fire cannot destroy it. Floods cannot wash it away. No locks nor bolts will ever be placed upon its doors, for no vicious person can ever enter that land where my dwelling stands, now almost completed and almost ready for me to enter in and abide in peace eternally, without fear of being ejected. There is a valley of deep shadow between the place where I live in California and that to which I shall journey in a very short time. I cannot reach my home in that City of Gold without passing through this dark valley of shadows. But I am not afraid because the best Friend I ever had went through the same valley long, long ago and drove away all its gloom. He has stuck by me through thick and thin, since we first became acquainted 55 years ago, and I hold His promise in printed form, never to forsake me or leave me alone. He will be with me as I walk through the valley of shadows, and I shall not lose my way when He is with me. I hope to hear your sermon on heaven next Sunday from my home in Los Angeles, California, but I have no assurance that I shall be able to do so. My ticket to heaven has no date marked for the journey, no return coupon, and no permit for baggage. Yes, I am all ready to go and I may not be here while you are talking next Sunday evening, but I shall meet you there some day.[1]

Oh, may that faithful man's tribe increase! Fix your eyes on the promise of heaven, and what you see will spoil you so much that you will be content to live as a pilgrim on earth with the patient expectation of your home with the Lord.

DATE:

KEY VERSE: "In my Father's house are many dwelling places; if it were not so, I would have told you; for I go to prepare a place for you. If I go and prepare a place for you, I will come again and receive you to Myself, that where I am, there you may be also" (John 14:2-3).

FOR FURTHER THOUGHT: How does the promise of an eternal home in heaven give you hope today? Do you need to hold anything with an open hand or let go of anything in order to lay up treasures in heaven?

MY RESPONSE:

HE WILL RETURN QUICKLY!

*And behold, I am coming quickly. Blessed
is he who heeds the words of the prophecy
of this book...Behold, I am coming quickly,
and my reward is with Me, to render to
every man according to what he has done...
He who testifies to these things says,"Yes, I am
coming quickly." Amen. Come, Lord Jesus.*

REVELATION 22:7,12,20

J esus is coming again, and He promises His return will happen quickly. This is comforting news for every weary sojourner here on earth, and it is the reason you should never walk with your face to the ground, but look to the sky. The Greek word translated "quickly" is *tachu* and means suddenly, swiftly, and soon. Jesus' return will occur instantaneously, in the twinkling of an eye.

As we near the end of our 30-day journey on hope and the promises of God, we will think about the last great promise of the Bible. He promises no less than three times, "I am coming quickly." This certain hope of seeing Him face-to-face is an eternal promise that can help you face the present and smile at the future.

After Jesus' ascension into heaven, two angels exhorted the eyewitnesses about the objective reality of Jesus' return. They said, "Men of Galilee, why do you stand looking into heaven? This Jesus, who was taken up from you into heaven, will come in the same way as you saw Him go into heaven" (Acts 1:11). Jesus is coming again. We see this promise repeated throughout Scripture. In Daniel's vision of the promised Messiah, "One like a Son of Man was coming," and He came "with the clouds of heaven" (Daniel 7:13). Jesus described His return as majestic and powerful, "For just as the lightning comes from the east and flashes even to the west, so will the coming of the Son of Man be" (Matthew 24:27).

The backdrop for the promise of the return of Christ is a powerful love story—God's love for those He created. The Lord wants to be with you, to live with you, and He desires your company forever. He wants you to have the sense that you are His beloved. He always desires your presence and your companionship. His eternal design is that you and He will share a home, walking and living together forever. In Leviticus 26:13, the Lord says, "I will also walk among you, and be your God, and you shall be my people." That promise, that great desire of God, is fulfilled in Revelation 21:3: "Behold, the tabernacle of God is among men, and He will dwell among them, and they shall be His people, and God Himself will be among them." The fulfillment of God's desire to live with His people eternally was made possible by the sacrifice of Jesus on the cross: "For God so loved the world, that He gave His only begotten Son, that whoever believes in Him shall not perish, but have eternal life" (John 3:16).

The cry of the universe is *Maranatha,* which means, "Our Lord, come!" This Greek word of Aramaic origin occurs only once in the Bible: Paul includes it in his climactic conclusion to his first letter to the Corinthian church (1 Corinthians 16:22). And Paul tells us in Romans 8:17-23, "I consider that the sufferings of this present time are not worthy to be compared with the glory that is to be revealed to us. For the anxious longing of the creation waits eagerly for the revealing of the sons of God…even we ourselves groan within ourselves, waiting eagerly for *our* adoption as sons, the redemption of our body." All of creation longs for the return of Christ, and the Lord looks forward to it Himself. We know that "for the joy set before Him," He endured the cross (Hebrews 12:2). That joy includes eternity with you.

Jesus Himself is coming back for you. He will not be sending an agent on His behalf to bring you home, but will receive you personally. He says in John 14:3, "I will come again and receive you to Myself, that where I am, there you may be also." Imagine that while Jesus was on earth, even before He was crucified, He had His mind on His return to bring you home to be with Him. Even if you experience death before His return, you can rest in the assurance that the "sting of death" is gone (1 Corinthians 15:54-57). You will be with Him instantaneously; to be absent from the body is to be present with the Lord (2 Corinthians 5:8).

A dear friend related to me the sudden homegoing of her husband, the instantaneous step from time into eternity.

> I had already gone to bed and was reading when he came in, laughing and kidding me. He got into bed and hugged me and kissed me and was holding me as I had turned back over to read. That's how we went to sleep at night. Suddenly there was an awful gasp and he was gone before I could even turn over to grab him!…He was only 62 and so strong physically; the shock was enormous, and I had to continually focus my mind on Scripture to carry me forward. What a journey it has been—a treasure beyond words to have such hope in the midst of such pain.

Once we, the bride of Christ, are in heaven, we will enjoy a wedding with our Bridegroom, the Lord Jesus Christ. "Let us rejoice and be glad and give the glory to Him, for the marriage of the Lamb has come and His bride has made herself ready" (Revelation 19:7). The celebration will include a wedding feast: "Blessed are those who are invited to the marriage supper of the Lamb…these are the true words of God" (Revelation 19:9). We will receive rewards, and one of the greatest rewards will be to hear those words, "Well done, good and faithful servant. You have been faithful over a little; I will set you over much. Enter into the joy of your master" (Matthew 25:21 ESV).

When you meet Jesus face-to-face, you will be changed. According to John, you will be like Jesus: "We know that when He appears, we will be like Him, because we will see Him just as He is" (1 John 3:2). Paul confirms this complete change.

> Behold, I tell you a mystery; we will not all sleep, but we will all be changed, in a moment, in the twinkling of an eye, at the last trumpet; for the trumpet will sound, and the dead will be raised imperishable, and we will be changed. For this perishable must put on the imperishable, and this mortal must put on immortality…death is swallowed up in victory…but thanks be to God, who gives us the victory through our Lord Jesus Christ" (1 Corinthians 15:51-57).

I dream of Joni Eareckson Tada running on a beach. I think of my mother able to walk easily hand-in-hand with the Lord. I think of Fanny Crosby, blind almost from birth, able to look fully on His wonderful face and see it with clarity. I think of Charles Spurgeon, his mind free from depression. I think of Thomas without any doubt. I think of Paul with no more thorn in the flesh.

Octavius Winslow speaks of the glorious nature of heaven:

> We shall no more see the King in his beauty as through a glass darkly, nor the good land very far off. With souls perfected in holiness, how clear will be the vision, how transparent the medium, how glorious the Object! There shall be no more night of mystery, no more night of obscurity, no more night of sin, no more night of weeping. No disease shall shade the intellect, no prejudice shall warp, no shock shall unhinge it. No adversity shall touch the heart, no bereavement shall sadden, no changed and chilled affection shall collapse it.[1]

And you can know that your future is secure. Someday your Prince will come. Paul affirms, "And so we shall always be with the Lord" (1 Thessalonians 4:17). That is the conclusion to the best of fairy tales: "And they lived happily ever after." But for you, redeemed by the blood of the Lamb, it is not a fairy tale; it is the real, true, and happy ending for the story of your life. You can know one thing that will always be true, one thing that nothing can touch, one thing that no amount of evil, suffering, or hardship can destroy. And that is your forever future with the Lord.

Sometimes I feel as if I cannot wait until forever. I always say to people, "Here, there, or in the air!" For me, *forever* means I will always see the Lord Jesus face-to-face. *Forever* means I will never be lonely again. *Forever* means I will have no more pain. *Forever* means I will have no more tears. *Forever* means I will have no more disappointment. *Forever* means I will have constant joy. *Forever* means perfection. What a comfort. What a joy. What a hope.

Forever is going to come quickly, according to the Lord. The time is short, and eternity is forever. Jesus encourages us to be on the alert, be ready, and be faithful to carry out the responsibilities He has given us until He comes (Matthew 24:42-51). Live with a heart that is ready to meet your Lord. How is this possible? Find the promise, embrace the promise, trust the promise, and live the promise. When you live the promises of God, you will be a radical disciple for the kingdom of God. Corrie ten Boom was a radical disciple. D.L. Moody was a radical disciple. And now is your time to be a radical disciple for the kingdom. I encourage you to find the promise, embrace the promise, trust the promise, and live the promise until you see your Lord.

You can know that you will always be with your Lord. Your Bridegroom, Jesus, is your great reward. He is greater than the crown you will receive and even greater than your new body. Being with Jesus will be your crowning glory. Perhaps that is why His return is called "the blessed hope." Paul tells Titus that we are "looking for the blessed hope and the appearing of the glory of our great God and Savior, Christ Jesus, who gave Himself for us to redeem us from every lawless deed, and to purify for Himself a people for His own possession" (Titus 2:13-14). This is your great hope—the blessed hope. Dear friend, write a check on the promise and hold on to it forever with patient expectation. And say, along with John, "Amen. Come, Lord Jesus."

Face to face with Christ my Savior,
Face to face—what will it be,
When with rapture I behold Him,
Jesus Christ, who died for me.

CARRIE E. BRECK

Lift up the trumpet and loud let it ring;
Jesus is coming again.
Cheer up, ye pilgrims, be joyful and sing;
Jesus is coming again.

JESSIE E. STROUT

The coming king is at the door,
Who once the cross for sinner bore,
But now righteous ones alone,
He comes to gather home.

F.E. BELDEN

Marvelous message we bring,
Glorious carol we sing,
Wonderful word of the King—
Jesus is coming again!

Coming again, coming again;
May be morning, may be noon,
May be evening and may be soon!
Coming again, coming again;
O what a wonderful day it will be—
Jesus is coming again![2]

JOHN W. PETERSON

My Response

DATE:

KEY VERSE: "He who testifies to these things says, 'Yes, I am coming quickly.' Amen. Come, Lord Jesus" (Revelation 22:20).

FOR FURTHER THOUGHT: How do the eternal promises we considered today give you hope? How will you apply what you have learned on this 30-day journey? What is the most important truth you have learned? What is your favorite promise and why? If someone were to ask you to explain why you have hope, what would you say?

MY RESPONSE:

Day Thirty

QUIET TIME
WEEK FIVE:
HOPE IN WHAT
JESUS SAYS

Let the word of Christ richly dwell within
you, with all wisdom teaching and
admonishing one another with psalms
and hymns and spiritual songs, singing
with thankfulness in your hearts to God.

COLOSSIANS 3:16

PREPARE YOUR HEART

You have spent the last 29 days thinking about hope and the promises of God. Your ability to hope is ultimately going to come down to this one thing: What will you do with the Word of the Lord? Will you stand on His promises as though your very life depended on it?

Russell Kelso Carter, an athlete, educator, rancher, preacher, and physician was surrounded by Christian influences throughout his life, but he ran away from the Lord for years. He thoroughly enjoyed the preaching of D.L. Moody and said the Lord's unlimited promises stood out like stars to him. And yet he refused to give himself to the Lord. He almost died because of heart problems, and through his illness, he knelt in his mother's room in Baltimore and committed himself to the Lord. One of the results of his commitment was the writing of this well-known and beloved hymn, "Standing on the Promises." As you begin your quiet time today, meditate on Carter's words on the promises of God. Ask yourself, *Am I standing on the promises of God?*

> Standing on the promises of Christ my King,
> Through eternal ages let His praises ring.
> "Glory in the highest," I will shout and sing,
> Standing on the promises of God.

> Standing on the promises that cannot fail
> When the howling storms of doubt and fear assail.
> By the living Word of God I shall prevail,
> Standing on the promises of God.

> Standing on the promises of Christ the Lord,
> Bound to Him eternally by love's strong cord,
> Overcoming daily with the Spirit's sword,
> Standing on the promises of God.

> Standing on the promises I cannot fall,
> Listening every moment to the Spirit's call,
> Resting in my Savior as my all in all,
> Standing on the promises of God.

> Standing, standing,
> Standing on the promises of God my Savior.
> Standing, standing,
> I'm standing on the promises of God.

READ AND STUDY GOD'S WORD

1. Paul encourages the Colossian church to "let the word of Christ richly dwell within you" (Colossians 3:16). Look at the following verses and record your insights related to what you can do with the Word of the Lord:

Psalm 119:11

Psalm 119:97

Psalm 119:148

Philippians 4:8

Colossians 3:16

2 Timothy 2:15

2. Summarize ways you can let the word of Christ richly dwell in you.

ADORE GOD IN PRAYER

Take time now to ask the Lord to give you a rich love for His Word and to teach you how to live in it that it may live in you.

YIELD YOURSELF TO GOD

Meditate on the following words written by D.L. Moody about the Bible:[1]

> A great many people seem to think that the Bible is out of date, that it is an old book, that it has passed its day. They say it was very good for the dark ages, and that there is some very good history in it, but it was not intended for the present time; we are living in a very enlightened age and men can get on very well without it; we have outgrown it. Now, you might just as well say that the sun, which has shone so long, is now so old that it is out of date, and that whenever a man builds a house he need not put any windows in it, because we have a newer light and a better light; we have gaslight and electric light. These are something new; and I would advise people, if they think the Bible is too old and worn

out, when they build houses, not to put windows in them, but just to light them with electric light; that is something new and that is what they are anxious for.

I thank God for the old Book. I thank God for this old promise. It is as sweet and fresh today as it has ever been. Thank God, none of these promises are out of date, or grown stale. They are as fresh, and vigorous, and young, and sweet as ever.

ENJOY HIS PRESENCE

Turn back to day 1 and read what you wrote in your letter to the Lord. As you think about this 30-day journey, summarize in a few sentences the most important truths you have learned. How will this journey make a difference in your life, and what will you carry with you?

REST IN HIS LOVE

"These things I have spoken to you so that My joy may be in you, and that your joy may be made full" (John 15:11).

APPENDIXES

Appendix 1

DISCUSSION
QUESTIONS

These questions are for people who share this 30-day journey together. This book is a great tool for talking together about hope and the promises of God. It also provides for a great 30-day preparation for one of the books of quiet times available from Quiet Time Ministries. God bless you as you help others discover hope and the magnificent promises of God.

Introduction

Use the introduction week to meet those in your group, hand out copies of this book, familiarize everyone with the topic of hope and God's promises, and play the introduction message (if you are using the weekly DVD messages for *Walking with the God Who Cares*). Begin your group time by asking, "What brought you to this 30-day journey? How did you hear about it?" Allow everyone to share. Then pass out the books and show those in your group how each week is organized, with a quiet time as the sixth day. Show your group all the information in the appendixes. You may want to encourage them to use these questions at the end of their week of reading and study to summarize what they have learned and prepare for the discussion. Tell them about the websites www.thegodwhocares.com, www.quiettime.org, www.cathsblog.com, and www.myquiettime.com, as well as the Quiet Time Café message board at www.quiettimecafe.com, where they can share insights online with others. Then, describe how you will structure your weekly meetings. You may want to use a sign-up sheet for snacks. You may also want to share prayer requests each week (use 3 x 5 cards for requests, and those in your group can take one of the requests for prayer during the week). Close in prayer.

Week One—Hope When There Is No Hope

DAY 1—Hope for My Deepest Darkness

1. Begin your time together in prayer. You may want to open your time of discussion by reading "At the Place of the Sea" by Annie Johnson Flint (just before the introduction).

2. Have someone read the verse at the beginning of each day. Ask each group member to share what it meant to him or her to spend daily time this last week thinking about hope.

3. How would you define hope?

4. What is the difference between the world's kind of hope and God's kind of hope described in the Bible?

5. What was your favorite statement in day 1? What challenged you? What encouraged you?

6. If you prayed the prayer to receive Christ for the first time, then you can know that the Lord Jesus lives in you and that you have been "born again to a living hope" (1 Peter 1:3).

DAY 2—When God Remembers You

1. In day 2 you saw that God will remember you in the storms in life. What does the word *remember* mean in this context?

2. How has God remembered you in a storm in your own life?

3. What did you learn from Noah's example? Talk about each of the insights from his example in day 2.

4. Where are you in your own journey of hope?

Day 3—Therefore I Have Hope

1. Why is Jeremiah such a good example of what it means to have hope?

2. What was your favorite quote from day 3?

Day 4—The University of Suffering

1. How have you experienced the university of suffering?

2. What did you learn about this university of suffering that will help you to have hope?

Day 5—Touching Heaven When Tested by Fire

1. What does it mean to touch heaven when tested by fire?

2. What did you learn from the example of Amy Carmichael?

3. What was your favorite quote from day 5?

Day 6—Quiet Time Week One: In Hope Against Hope

1. On day 6 you had the opportunity to experience a quiet time based on the example of Abraham. What does it mean to have a "hope against hope" kind of belief?

2. What meant the most to you from Abraham's life?

3. What quote, verse, or insight encouraged you the most this week?

Week Two: A Living Hope in the Promises

Day 7—The Magnificent Promises of God

1. Introduce today's discussion by doing a quick review of what you discussed last week. This will be of special benefit to those who are just joining your group. You might review by

sharing what hope is all about—that it means **Holding On** with **P**atient **E**xpectation. You might share how this kind of hope is different from simply wishing that something will happen. The Christian hope is focused on the promises in God's Word. As you lead your group through a discussion of each day in week 2, you may want to have someone read the verse at the beginning of each day.

2. In day 7 we looked at the promises of God. What is a promise? How would you define it or describe it?

3. Why is a promise of God like a check that you write? How did that picture help you to understand the promises of God?

4. What was your favorite insight about the promises of God?

5. Why do you need the promises of God in your own life?

Day 8—Find the Promise

1. On day 8 you learned how to find the promise. Why do the promises make you so rich?

2. What will help you find the promises in God's Word? Notice the 31 promises in appendix 2.

Day 9—Embrace the Promise

1. In day 9 you learned how to embrace the promise. Why is surrender necessary if you are to embrace the promise? What does surrender to the Lord mean? Why is surrender a good thing?

2. What did you learn about claiming a promise and what that really means?

3. What did you learn from the example of Corrie ten Boom?

4. You learned about the importance of studying the promise. What are some ways to study the promise? What tools will you use to help you study the promises of God?

5. How does writing out what you have learned in your journal or *Quiet Time Notebook* help you?

6. How did this day challenge you in your own relationship with the Lord?

Day 10—Trust the Promise

1. In day 10 you looked at trusting the promise. Why is it necessary to trust the promise, and how can you trust the promise?

2. How does writing a check on the promise help you see what it means to trust the promise? Did you write a check on a promise this week, and if so, what promise did the Lord give you?

3. Has the Lord ever brought a promise to your mind that you trusted in your situation?

4. How does prayer help you trust the promises of God?

5. Where do you need the promises of God in your own life today?

Day 11—Live the Promise

1. In day 11 you thought about what it means to live the promise. Once you have found the promise, embraced the promise, and trusted the promise, what does it mean to live the promise?

2. What is hope's reward? In what way was Corrie ten Boom an example of what the love of God can do?

3. How does Amy Carmichael's example help you in understanding the choice we have in suffering?

4. What was your favorite quote from day 11?

Day 12—Quiet Time Week Two: Hope That Does Not Disappoint

1. Why might the saying "Hope does not disappoint" be so difficult to comprehend?

2. How can a trial actually lead to hope?

3. How did this week influence your thinking and understanding of hope and the promises of God?

4. What was your favorite insight, quote, or verse from your reading and study this week? What have you thought about most this week as you have engaged in this 30-day journey?

Week Three: Hope in Who He Is

DAY 13—Hope in the Lord

1. In the last two weeks we have been talking about hope and the promises of God. We have seen a difference between wishing something will happen and the kind of hope that soars on the wings of the promises of God. Last week we talked about finding, embracing, trusting, and living the promise. As we begin today, what is the most important thing you've learned so far in this 30-day journey? As you lead your group through a discussion of each day in week 3, you may want to have someone read the verse at the beginning of each day.

2. In day 13 you saw how you can find hope in the Lord. How does knowing who God is help move you from despair to hope in life?

3. What did you learn from the illustration about the weaving?

4. What was your favorite truth about God? Which aspect of His character means the most to you today?

5. How did John Bunyan endure his prison experience?

6. What was your favorite quote?

DAY 14—He Is Able

1. In day 14 we looked more deeply at a promise about the character of God found in Ephesians 3:20-21. Why is this such a great promise in Scripture? What did you learn from this promise about God?

2. How can a valley or wilderness become a place of hope?

3. What did you learn from the life of Annie Johnson Flint?

Day 15—The Exact Explanation of God

1. According to all that you read in day 15, what is the best way to know what God is like?

2. What did you learn about Jesus in this day's reading?

3. How does Jesus explain God?

4. What was the purpose of Jesus' death on the cross?

Day 16—Jesus Wept

1. In day 16 you read about two important words in Scripture: *Jesus wept*. What is the significance of Jesus' weeping?

2. What did you learn about the heart of God? How did the Isaiah passage help you understand God's heart?

3. What was the most important truth you learned in day 16?

4. How did what you learned in this day's reading give you hope and encouragement in the storms of life?

5. What do you look forward to in eternity?

Day 17—He Is Your Wonderful Counselor

1. In day 17 you looked at Jesus as your Wonderful Counselor. Why is He called the Wonderful Counselor?

2. Can you describe a time when you had run to Him as your Wonderful Counselor? What difference did it make in your situation?

3. What is your favorite truth about wisdom?

4. Where can we find wisdom from God?

Day 18—Quiet Time Week Three: Hope in Jesus Your Savior

1. In day 18, you spent time with the Lord, looking at Him as your Savior. Why is knowing Him as Savior such a life-changing truth? Why does it give you hope?

2. What was your favorite quote or insight from your quiet time?

3. What was the most important idea or truth you learned from your time thinking about hope in who God is this week?

Week Four: Hope in What He Does
DAY 19—He Works in Me

1. We have been looking these last four weeks at hope and the promises of God. This week we looked at hope in promises related to what the Lord does. As you lead your group through a discussion of each day in week 4, you may want to have someone read the verse at the beginning of each day.

   As you spent this week thinking about what God does, what was the most important thing you learned? How did God speak to you this week?

2. What did you learn from the promise about God's work in your life?

3. According to the Word, what is God making you? What difference would living like a saint make in your life?

4. What did you learn from the words of Wuest on pages 152–153?

5. What happened in John Newton's life, and how did that give you hope about how God can work in your life?

DAY 20—He Intercedes for Me

1. In day 20 you learned that Jesus is your Intercessor. How does that promise give you hope?

2. What does the fact that He intercedes for you mean for your life?

3. How do you need His intercession in your life right now?

DAY 21—He Strengthens Me

1. In day 21 you looked at the strength of the Lord in your life. Why do you need the strength and power of the Lord?

2. Have you ever faced an impossible task that required you to rely on the Lord? What happened?

3. What does it take to rely on the power of the Lord in your life? How did the examples in this day's reading help you?

Day 22—He Blesses Me

1. Day 22 begins with this statement: "You are blessed by God with every spiritual blessing." What does that mean?

2. What does the blessing of God depend on?

3. What are some of the spiritual blessings that every believer in Christ has?

4. What did you learn from the example of Frances Ridley Havergal?

Day 23—He Produces Fruit in Me

1. In day 23 you looked at how the Lord produces fruit in you. What does it mean to abide in Christ?

2. Why is abiding in Christ necessary if you are to bear fruit?

3. What does it mean to bear fruit?

4. What would you like to be remembered for as a result of your life on earth?

Day 24—Quiet Time Week Four: Hope in What Jesus Has Done

1. Why is the cross so important in your life?

2. What did you learn about the cross?

3. What was the most important truth you learned from your quiet time?

4. Would you like to share a favorite verse, quote, or insight from the entire week?

Week Five: Hope in What He Says

Day 25—The Word of God Lasts Forever

1. What a journey we have had exploring how to walk with the God who cares. You have spent 30 days focusing on hope

and the magnificent promises of God. This is not really an ending but a beginning as you apply all that you have learned about God's promises.

As you have now finished reading this book, what is the most important thing you've learned as a result of the journey? How will this book and its emphasis on the promises of God make a difference in your life? How has it changed your view of hope in the midst of trials in your own life?

2. In day 25 you had the opportunity to think about the great value of the Word of God. What decision does every person need to make about the Bible, and why?

3. How will building your life on the foundation of the Word make a difference in your life?

4. What must we do with the Word of God in order for it to be our foundation in life?

Day 26—Your Times Are in His Hand

1. In day 26 we looked at the promise in Psalm 31:15 that says, "My times are in His hand." How does this promise bring hope to those of us who suffer?

2. What truths can you know because your times are in His hand?

3. What was your favorite quote or insight from the reading?

Day 27—The Audience of One

1. In day 27, you read about ministry and the audience of one. What does it mean to live for the audience of one?

2. Who has been a strong example for you in ministry?

3. What has God entrusted to you in your own life? How will what you've read today help you and encourage you?

4. Why is living for the audience of one a challenge in life? What will help us live for the audience of one?

Day 28—A Place for You

1. Day 28 begins this way: "Your real home is in heaven." What does that mean, and what can you know about your real home?

2. How can the promise of heaven bring hope in life?

3. Do you need to hold anything with an open hand or let go of anything in order to lay up treasures in heaven?

Day 29—He Will Return Quickly

1. In day 29 you looked at the return of Jesus Christ. How do the eternal promises related to the return of Christ encourage you and give you hope?

2. What do you look forward to in eternity?

Day 30—Quiet Time Week Five: Hope in What Jesus Says

1. What's so great about standing on the promises of God?

2. How can you let the word of Christ dwell in you richly? What did you learn from the different verses you looked at?

3. As you think about your journey over the last 30 days, what has been most significant to you?

4. What is the most important thing you have learned in this 30-day journey? What will you take with you from this time?

5. Who was your favorite example? What was your favorite verse or favorite quote?

6. Would you like to share anything else as a result of your 30-day journey? Close in prayer.

THIRTY-ONE PROMISES TO GIVE YOU HOPE

⁓∾

The Bible contains many wonderful promises of God. Here are 31 of the best for you to "write the check" on when you need them. Memorize each one so they will always be available for you at any time. You might want to meditate on one each day for the next 31 days. You might even look at each verse in other translations, commentaries, and the *Treasury of Scripture Knowledge*. If you have the *Quiet Time Notebook*, you can use a Read and Study page or a Journal page for each verse.

When you are tempted...

> No temptation has overtaken you but such as is common to man; and God is faithful, who will not allow you to be tempted beyond what you are able, but with the temptation will provide the way of escape also, so that you will be able to endure it (1 Corinthians 10:13).

When you sin...

> If we confess our sins, He is faithful and righteous to forgive us our sins and to cleanse us from all unrighteousness (1 John 1:9).

When you are worried and anxious...

> Be anxious for nothing, but in everything by prayer and supplication with thanksgiving let your requests be made known to God. And the peace of God, which surpasses all comprehension, will guard your hearts and your minds in Christ Jesus (Philippians 4:6-7).

When you need encouragement about prayer...

> This is the confidence which we have before Him, that, if we ask anything according to His will, He hears us. And if we know that He hears us in whatever we ask, we know that we have the requests which we have asked from Him (1 John 5:14-15).

When you need motivation to pray...

> Call to Me and I will answer you, and I will tell you great and mighty things, which you do not know (Jeremiah 33:3).

When you feel weak...

> Do you not know? Have you not heard? The Everlasting God, the LORD, the Creator of the ends of the earth does not become weary or tired. His understanding is inscrutable. He gives strength to the weary, and to him who lacks might He increases power. Though youths grow weary and tired, and vigorous young men stumble badly, yet those who wait for the LORD will gain new strength; they will mount up with wings like eagles, they will run and not get tired, they will walk and not become weary (Isaiah 40:28-31).

When you are tired...

> Come to Me, all who are weary and heavy-laden, and I will give you rest. Take my yoke upon you and learn from Me, for I am gentle and humble in heart, and you will find rest for your souls. For my yoke is easy and My burden is light (Matthew 11:28-30).

When you get too busy...

Cease striving and know that I am God (Psalm 46:10).

When you are sad...

For His anger is but for a moment, his favor is for a lifetime. Weeping may last for the night, but a shout of joy comes in the morning (Psalm 30:5).

When you need rejuvenation...

Times of refreshing may come from the presence of the Lord (Acts 3:19).

When you have suffered for a long time...

And I heard a loud voice from the throne saying, "Behold, the tabernacle of God is among men, and He will dwell among them, and they shall be His people, and God Himself will be among them, and He will wipe away every tear from their eyes; and there will no longer be any death; there will no longer be any mourning, or crying, or pain; the first things have passed away." And He who sits on the throne said, "Behold, I am making all things new." And He said, "Write, for these words are faithful and true" (Revelation 21:3-5).

When you are going through a time of change...

Do not call to mind the former things, or ponder things of the past. Behold, I will do something new, now it will spring forth; will you not be aware of it? I will even make a roadway in the wilderness, rivers in the desert (Isaiah 43:18-19).

When you don't understand...

"For My thoughts are not your thoughts, nor are your ways My ways," declares the LORD. "For as the heavens are higher than the earth, so are My ways higher than your ways and My thoughts than your thoughts" (Isaiah 55:8-9).

When you need the Word of God...

> For as the rain and the snow come down from heaven, and do not return there without watering the earth and making it bear and sprout, and furnishing seed to the sower and bread to the eater; so will My word be which goes forth from My mouth; it will not return to Me empty, without accomplishing what I desire, and without succeeding in the matter for which I sent it (Isaiah 55:10-11).

When you need encouragement to trust the Lord...

> Thus says the LORD, "Cursed is the man who trusts in mankind and makes flesh his strength, and whose heart turns away from the LORD. For he will be like a bush in the desert and will not see when prosperity comes, but will live in stony wastes in the wilderness, a land of salt without inhabitant. Blessed is the man who trusts in the LORD and whose trust is the LORD. For he will be like a tree planted by the water, that extends its roots by a stream and will not fear when the heat comes; but its leaves will be green, and it will not be anxious in a year of drought nor cease to yield fruit" (Jeremiah 17:5-8).

When you are losing hope...

> This I recall to my mind, therefore I have hope. The LORD's lovingkindnesses indeed never cease, for His compassions never fail. They are new every morning; great is Your faithfulness. "The LORD is my portion," says my soul, "Therefore I have hope in Him" (Lamentations 3:21-24).

When you need to wait...

> Trust in the LORD and do good; dwell in the land and cultivate faithfulness. Delight yourself in the LORD, and He will give you the desires of your heart. Commit your way to the LORD, trust also in Him, and He will do it. He will bring forth your righteousness as the light and your judgment as the noonday. Rest in the LORD and wait patiently for

Him; do not fret because of him who prospers in his way, because of the man who carries out wicked schemes. Cease from anger and forsake wrath; do not fret; it leads only to evildoing. For evildoers will be cut off, but those who wait for the LORD, they will inherit the land (Psalm 37:3-9).

When you feel that your life is going nowhere...

"For I know the plans that I have for you," declares the LORD, "plans for welfare and not for calamity to give you a future and a hope" (Jeremiah 29:11).

When things aren't working out...

And we know that God causes all things to work together for good to those who love God, to those who are called according to His purpose (Romans 8:28).

When you don't feel loved...

I have loved you with an everlasting love; therefore I have drawn you with lovingkindness (Jeremiah 31:3).

When you feel alone...

Who will separate us from the love of Christ? Will tribulation, or distress, or persecution, or famine, or nakedness, or peril, or sword? Just as it is written, "For Your sake we are being put to death all day long; we were considered as sheep to be slaughtered." But in all these things we overwhelmingly conquer through Him who loved us. For I am convinced that neither death, or life, nor angels, nor principalities, nor things present, nor things to come, nor powers, nor height, nor depth, nor any other created thing, will be able to separate us from the love of God, which is in Christ Jesus our Lord (Romans 8:35-39).

When you need help...

Do not fear, for I am with you; do not anxiously look about

you, for I am your God. I will strengthen you, surely I will help you, surely I will uphold you with My righteous right hand (Isaiah 41:10).

When you feel forgotten...

Can a woman forget her nursing child and have no compassion on the son of her womb? Even these may forget, but I will not forget you. Behold, I have inscribed you on the palms of My hands; Your walls are continually before Me (Isaiah 49:15-16).

When you need the grace of God...

For we do not have a high priest who cannot sympathize with our weaknesses, but One who has been tempted in all things as we are, yet without sin. Therefore, let us draw near with confidence to the throne of grace, so that we may receive mercy and find grace to help in time of need (Hebrews 4:15-16).

When you are suffering...

After you have suffered for a little while, the God of all grace, who called you to His eternal glory in Christ, will Himself perfect, confirm, strengthen and establish you (1 Peter 5:10).

When you suffer for your faith in Christ...

Beloved, do not be surprised at the fiery ordeal among you, which comes upon you for your testing, as though some strange thing were happening to you; but to the degree that you share the sufferings of Christ, keep on rejoicing, so that also at the revelation of His glory you may rejoice with exultation. If you are reviled for the name of Christ, you are blessed, because the Spirit of glory and of God rests on you (1 Peter 4:12-14).

When you have a need...

And my God will supply all your needs according to His riches in glory in Christ Jesus (Philippians 4:19).

When you need strength for an impossible task...

> I can do all things through Him who strengthens me (Philippians 4:13).

When you can't let go of guilt...

> Therefore there is now no condemnation for those who are in Christ Jesus. For the law of the Spirit of life in Christ Jesus has set you free from the law of sin and of death (Romans 8:1-2).

When you are losing heart...

> Therefore we do not lose heart, but though our outer man is decaying, yet our inner man is being renewed day by day. For momentary, light affliction is producing for us an eternal weight of glory far beyond all comparison, while we look not at the things which are seen, but at the things which are not seen; for the things which are seen are temporal, but the things which are not seen are eternal (2 Corinthians 4:16-18).

When you need the hope of eternity...

> There will no longer be any curse; and the throne of God and of the Lamb will be in it, and His bond-servants will serve Him; they will see His face, and His name will be on their foreheads. And there will no longer be any night; and they will not have need of the light of a lamp nor the light of the sun, because the Lord God will illumine them; and they will reign forever and ever (Revelation 22:3-5).

Treasure from God's Promises in His Word

Date_____

*This promise is for*_____   _____

Promise

_____

_____

_____

_____

_____

Memo—occasions and dates I've drawn on this promise from God's Word:

"All Scripture is inspired by God" (2 Timothy 3:16).

"For as many as are the promises of God, in Him they are yes" (2 Corinthians 1:20).

"The grass withers, the flower fades, but the word of our God stands forever" (Isaiah 40:8).

"Heaven and earth will pass away, but My words will not pass away" (Matthew 24:35).

"Your word is a lamp to my feet and a light for my path" (Psalm 119:105).

Appendix 3

RECOMMENDED READING

Biographies and Autobiographies

Amma by Elizabeth R. Skoglund

A Chance to Die by Elisabeth Elliot

D.L. Moody on Spiritual Leadership by Steve Miller

The Five Silent Years of Corrie ten Boom by Pamela Rosewell Moore

The Hiding Place by Corrie ten Boom

Joni by Joni Eareckson

Letters of Samuel Rutherford by Samuel Rutherford

Life Lessons from the Hiding Place by Pamela Rosewell Moore

Living with the Giants by Warren W. Wiersbe

The Shadow of the Almighty by Elisabeth Elliot

The Shadow of the Broad Brim by Richard Ellsworth Day

Spurgeon on Spiritual Leadership by Steve Miller

A Step Further by Joni Eareckson

Tramp for the Lord by Corrie ten Boom

THE CHARACTER AND ATTRIBUTES OF GOD

The Existence and Attributes of God by Charnock
The God of All Comfort by Hannah Whitall Smith
Knowing God by J.I. Packer
The Knowledge of the Holy by A.W. Tozer
The Pursuit of God by A.W. Tozer

THE PROMISES OF GOD

Daily Light for Every Day by Samuel Bagster and Anne Graham Lotz
God's Promises for Every Day, complied by W Publishing Group, 1996
God's Special Promises to Me by Clift Richards with Lloyd Hildebrand
Knowing God's Will series by Lee Roberts
The One Year Book of Bible Promises by Ruth Calkin

SUFFERING AND HOPE

Baffled to Fight Better by Oswald Chambers
Beside Still Waters by Charles Haddon Spurgeon
The Blessings of Brokenness by Charles Stanley
Christian Disciplines by Oswald Chambers
The Christian's Secret of a Happy Life by Hannah Whitall Smith
Don't Wrestle, Just Nestle by Corrie ten Boom
The God of All Comfort by Hannah Whitall Smith
Gold by Moonlight by Amy Carmichael
Help Heavenward by Octavius Winslow
The Hidden Smile of God by John Piper
Hope Again by Charles Swindoll
How Long, O Lord? by D.A. Carson
A Lifting Up for the Downcast by William Bridge
The North Face of God by Ken Gire
Spiritual Depression by Martyn Lloyd-Jones
Springs in the Valley by Mrs. Charles Cowman
Streams in the Desert by Mrs. Charles Cowman
Under His Wings by Ole Hallesby

Appendix 4

HOW TO FIND
HOPE IN THE
PROMISES OF GOD

FIND THE PROMISE

- Set aside a time, determine a place, and have a plan each day to spend quiet time alone with the Lord.

- Choose a Bible reading plan to Read and Study God's Word each day.

- Choose some devotional books that will help you learn the promises of God.

- To find a promise, always look for a verse that teaches you something about who God is, what He does, or what He says (His character, His works, and His Word).

- Consider the context of the verse to understand what God is promising you.

EMBRACE THE PROMISE

- Study the promise to gain insight into its meaning.
- Write out what you have learned about the promise in your journal or *Quiet Time Notebook.*
- Yield to the promise with a heart of surrender.
- Watch eagerly to see what God is going to do in your life and in the lives of others.

TRUST THE PROMISE

- Memorize the promise.
- Pray the promise.
- Personalize the promise.
- Write a check on the promise—attach your name to God's promise and turn it over to the Lord.

LIVE THE PROMISE

- Live and walk by faith according to what you know to be true in the promises of God.
- Look for God's love, the reward of hope, as you live by the promises of God.

I have learned these three acrostics in my own quiet time with the Lord, and I pray that they will help you find hope in the promises of God:

Hope

Holding **O**n with **P**atient **E**xpectation

Trust

Total **R**eliance **U**nder **S**tress and **T**rial

Wait

    Watching **A**lways **I** **T**rust Him

The following acrostic is from Corrie ten Boom:

Faith

    Fantastic **A**dventure **I**n **T**rusting **H**im

NOTES

DAY 1—*HOPE FOR MY DEEPEST DARKNESS*

1. Corrie ten Boom, *Tramp for the Lord* (Old Tappen, NJ: Fleming H. Revell, 1974), 4.
2. Kenneth S. Wuest, *Word Studies in the Greek New Testament* (Grand Rapids: Wm. B. Eerdmans Publishing Company, 1973), 2:35.
3. Corrie ten Boom, *The Hiding Place* (Grand Rapids: Chosen Books, 1971), 159.
4. Annie Johnson Flint, *Best-Loved Poems* (Toronto: Evangelical Publishers, n.d.), 79.

DAY 2—*WHEN GOD REMEMBERS YOU*

1. Ronald Youngblood, *How It All Began* (Ventura, CA: Regal Books, 1980), 119.

DAY 3—*THEREFORE I HAVE HOPE*

1. John Henry Jowett, *The School of Calvary* (London: James Clarke & Co., 1910), 58-59.

DAY 4—*THE UNIVERSITY OF SUFFERING*

1. D.A. Carson, *How Long, O Lord?* (Grand Rapids: Baker Academic, 1990), 42.
2. Cleon Rogers and Fritz Rienecker, *A Linguistic Key to the Greek New Testament* (Grand Rapids: Zondervan, 1976), 705.

DAY 5—*TOUCHING HEAVEN WHEN TESTED BY FIRE*

1. Amy Carmichael, *Gold by Moonlight* (Fort Washington, PA: CLC Publications, 1995), 153-154. For more information or to order this and other books by Amy Carmichael, call 800-659-1240.
2. Carmichael, 154.
3. D.A. Carson, *How Long, O Lord?* (Grand Rapids: Baker Academic, 1990), 191.

DAY 6—*QUIET TIME WEEK ONE: IN HOPE AGAINST HOPE*

1. Barclay Newman and Eugene Nida, *A Translator's Handbook on Paul's Letter to the Romans* (New York: United Bible Societies, 1973), 86-87.
2. C.E.B. Cranfield, *The Epistle to the Romans: Romans 1–8* (Edinburgh: T & T Clark Limited, 1975), 245-246.
3. Catherine Marshall, ed., *The Prayers of Peter Marshall* (New York: McGraw Hill, 1954), 13.

DAY 7—*THE MAGNIFICENT PROMISES OF GOD*

1. Barclay Newman and Eugene Nida, *A Translator's Handbook on Paul's Second Letter to Timothy* (New York: United Bible Societies, n.d.), n.p.
2. Mrs. Charles Cowman, *Streams in the Desert* (Grand Rapids: Zondervan, 1999). See the entry for March 8.

DAY 8—*FIND THE PROMISE*

1. John Henry Jowett, *The Epistles of St. Peter* (Grand Rapids: Kregel Publications, 1970), 221-222.
2. Ibid., 222.
3. Catherine Martin, *Six Secrets to a Powerful Quiet Time* (Eugene, OR: Harvest House Publishers, 2006).

DAY 9—*EMBRACE THE PROMISE*

1. Ken Gire, *The North Face of God* (Wheaton: Tyndale House Publishers, 2005), 60.
2. D.A. Carson, *How Long, O Lord?* (Grand Rapids: Baker Academic, 1990), 225.
3. Ibid., 239.
4. Pamela Rosewell Moore, *The Five Silent Years of Corrie ten Boom* (Grand Rapids: Zondervan, 1986), 47.

DAY 10—*TRUST THE PROMISE*

1. Charles Spurgeon, *Faith's Checkbook* (Wheaton: Moody Publishers, 1987). From the introduction.

2. Cited in Elizabeth R. Skoglund, *Amma* (Grand Rapids: Baker Book House, 1994), 210.

DAY 11—*LIVE THE PROMISE*

1. Hannah Whitall Smith, *The Christian's Secret of a Happy Life* (Urichsville, OH: Barbour Publishing, 2006), n.p.
2. Amy Carmichael, *Toward Jerusalem* (Fort Washington, PA: CLC Publications, 1989), 10. Used by permission. For more information or to order this and other books by Amy Carmichael, call 800-659-1240.

DAY 12—*QUIET TIME WEEK TWO: HOPE THAT DOES NOT DISAPPOINT*

1. C.E.B. Cranfield, *The Epistle to the Romans: Romans 1–8* (Edinburgh: T & T Clark Publishers, 1975), 261-262.
2. Kenneth S. Wuest, *Word Studies in the Greek New Testament* (Chicago: Moody Press, 1955), 1:78-79.

DAY 13—*HOPE IN THE LORD*

1. Octavius Winslow, *Help Heavenward* (Carlisle, PA: Banner of Truth Trust, 2000), 50.
2. Corrie ten Boom, *Each New Day* (Grand Rapids: Revell, 2005), 53.
3. A.W. Tozer, *The Knowledge of the Holy* (New York: Harper & Row, 1961), 10-11.
4. Hannah Whitall Smith, *The Christian's Secret of a Happy Life* (Urichsville, OH: Barbour Publishing, 2006), n.p.
5. Cited in John Piper, *The Hidden Smile of God* (Wheaton: Crossway Books, 2001), 61.

DAY 14—*HE IS ABLE*

1. Annie Johnson Flint, *Best-Loved Poems* (Toronto: Evangelical Publishers, n.d.), 38.

DAY 16—*JESUS WEPT*

1. F.B. Meyer, *Devotional Commentary* (Wheaton: Tyndale House Publishers, 1989), 469.
2. John F. Mogabgab, "The Gift of Tears," *Weavings: A Journal of the Christian Spiritual Life*, 15, no. 2:3.

DAY 17—*HE IS YOUR WONDERFUL COUNSELOR*

1. Matthew Henry, *Matthew Henry's Commentary on the Whole Bible* (Peabody, MA: Hendrickson, 1996). See commentary on James 1:2.
2. J.I. Packer, *Knowing God* (Downers Grove, IL: InterVarsity Press, 1973), 97.

DAY 18—QUIET TIME WEEK THREE: HOPE IN JESUS YOUR SAVIOR

1. Charles Spurgeon, *Morning and Evening* (New Kensington, PA: Whitaker House, 2001). See the evening entry for November 27.

DAY 19—HE WORKS IN ME

1. Kenneth Wuest, Word Studies in the Greek New Testament (Grand Rapids: Wm. B. Eerdmans Publishing company, 1973), 2:74-75. All rights reserved. Used by permission of the publisher.

DAY 20—HE INTERCEDES FOR ME

1. A.B. Simpson, *The Christ Life* (Camp Hill, PA: Christian Publications, 1980), 31.
2. F.B. Meyer, *The Way into the Holiest* (Grand Rapids: Baker Book House, 1951), 131.

DAY 21—HE STRENGTHENS ME

1. Cited in Steve Miller, *D.L. Moody on Spiritual Leadership,* (Chicago: Moody Press, 2004), 102.
2. J.I. Packer, *Knowing God* (Downers Grove, IL: InterVarsity Press, 1973), 227.

DAY 22—HE BLESSES ME

1. Kenneth S. Wuest, *Word Studies in the Greek New Testament* (Grand Rapids: Wm. B. Eerdmans Publishing Company, 1953), 1:27. Used by permission.
2. Ruth Paxson, *Rivers of Living Water* (London: Marshall, Morgan & Scott, 1930), 47-49.
3. Cited in Mrs. Victor Raymond Edman, *They Found the Secret* (Grand Rapids: Zondervan, 1960), 66. Used by permission.

DAY 24—QUIET TIME WEEK FOUR: HOPE IN WHAT JESUS HAS DONE

1. Catherine Marshall, ed., *The Prayers of Peter Marshall* (New York: McGraw Hill Book Company, 1954), 25.
2. D.A. Carson, *How Long, O Lord?* (Grand Rapids: Baker Academic, 1990), 183.

DAY 26—YOUR TIMES ARE IN HIS HAND

1. Cited in Elizabeth R. Skoglund, *Amma* (Grand Rapids: Baker Book House, 1994), 204.
2. D.A. Carson, *How Long, O Lord?* (Grand Rapids: Baker Academic, 1990), 174.
3. Skoglund, 159.
4. Pamela Rosewell Moore, *The Five Silent Years of Corrie ten Boom* (Grand Rapids: Zondervan, 1986), 183.

DAY 27—*THE AUDIENCE OF ONE*

1. Matthew Woodley, "An Audience of One," *Discipleship Journal,* March–April 2001.
2. A.W. Tozer, *Men Who Met God* (Camp Hill, PA: Christian Publications, 1986), 32-35.
3. Quoted in Elisabeth Elliot, *Shadow of the Almighty* (San Francisco: Harper & Row, 1958), 11.
4. Ibid., n.p.

DAY 28—*A PLACE FOR YOU*

1. Paul Lee Tan, *Encyclopedia of 7700 Illustrations* (Rockville, MD: Assurance Publishers, 1979, 1984), 545-46. Used by permission.

DAY 29—*HE WILL RETURN QUICKLY*

1. Octavius Winslow, *Help Heavenward* (Carlisle, PA: Banner of Truth, 2000), 59.
2. John W. Peterson, © 1957, renewed 1985 by John W. Petersen Music Company. All rights reserved. Used by permission.

DAY 30—*QUIET TIME WEEK FIVE: HOPE IN WHAT JESUS SAYS*

1. Quoted in Steve Miller, *D.L. Moody on Spiritual Leadership* (Chicago: Moody Press, 2004), 117-118.

ACKNOWLEDGMENTS

Thank you to my beloved husband, David, who is my strong support and is one of the great joys of my life. Thank you, David, for your incredible skill in editing, video production, website design, and a thousand other things. You are the most brilliant man I know, and you give me such unconditional love and deep wisdom. Thank you for being the love of my life.

Thank you to my mother, Elizabeth Snyder, for teaching me so much about hope with your words and your example. And thank you to my dad, Robert Snyder, for listening to me and loving me at every stage in this great adventure called life. Rob and Tania, thank you for your love and support. Robert, thank you for being my brother and encouraging me in all that God has called me to do. Tania, thank you for being such a computer expert whom I can consult anytime. Christopher, you are a wonderful young man, and I am so proud of you. Kayla, you are my bright shining star, and I am asking the Lord to do great and mighty things through you. I loved watching you walk back and forth across the stage as though you were speaking to a crowd just like your aunt, and I pray that someday you will do it for real. Thank you, Eloise, for being my mother-in-law and encouraging me to be strong in the Lord.

This book is about walking with God and finding hope in His promises. I am so thankful for my dear friends who have helped me to look to the Lord and His promises in my trials. Andy Graybill, you have been so faithful to give me just the right verses when I have been in the dark night of the soul. Bev Trupp, I am so thankful for your wisdom and for cheering me on when the Lord gives me a big idea. Cindy Clark, you have shared so much with me in Quiet Time Ministries, and I am so thankful that you believe the Lord for big things in this race the Lord has set before us. Conni Hudson, thank you for encouraging me with God's perspective when I have gone through difficult times. Shirley Peters, I am so encouraged when you share what the Lord is teaching you in His Word. Kelly Abeyratne, thank you for praying for me on my pilgrimage of the heart. Thank you to Julie Airis for writing e-mails to me that contain words of hope just when I need them. Thank you to Helen Peck for sharing my journey with the Lord for so many years. Thank you also to Stefanie Kelly, Myra Murphy, Betty Mann, and Kathleen Otremba, who encourage me to run my race well.

A special thank you to my assistant, Kayla Branscum, who tirelessly serves the Lord with me in this ministry. Kayla, you are so incredibly gifted and organized. I am so thankful that the Lord called you to this ministry. Thank you for sharing my heart and for reaching out to thousands as you print books, send out orders, organize speaking engagements, and speak to leaders throughout the United States and the world. Thank you especially for your hard work in organizing the pilot of *Walking with the God Who Cares* and for obtaining all the permissions.

Serving with the Quiet Time Ministries staff team is such a joy. A special thank you to Paula Zillmer for all your tireless work at our Resource and Training Center.

Thank you to the board of directors of Quiet Time Ministries—David Martin, Conni Hudson, Shirley Peters, and Jane Lyons—for joining me on this journey of ministry during our stay on earth. I have been so excited to see the Lord open doors that we could have never imagined. Thank you to the *Enriching Your Quiet Time* magazine writers and editors who have helped me develop the ideas for this book through articles and quiet times: managing editor Shirley Peters and writers Conni Hudson, Cay Hough, and Maurine Cromwell. Thank you to those men and women who partner with me in Quiet Time Ministries through your faithful prayers and gifts. I am blessed to serve together with you.

Thank you also to the staff at Southwest Community Church. A special thank you to Shelley, my assistant, who shares my love for serving the women at our church. Thank you also to the women of Southwest who are such an encouragement to me. Thank you to Pastor Bob Thune for your commitment to preach the Word of God. And a special thank you to our adult ministries staff team: Pastor Mark Wold, Pastor Jim Smoke, Pastor Pablo Cachon, Caroline Sharpe, and Shelley Smith.

Thank you to those who piloted *Walking with the God Who Cares:* Conni Hudson, Jodi Adams, Kayla Branscum, Melissa Brown, Ceil Burns, Sheila Chadwick, Cindy Clark, Donna Delahanty, Francene Fisher, Jean Gunderson, Carolyn Haynes, Joan Hill, Dawn Ivie, Davida Kreisler, Sally Leachman, Kay McCann, Shirley Peters, Sarah Rochford, Paula Zillmer, Bev Trupp, Lori Everson, Diane Kohler, Linda McClain, Carol Kendall, Kenn Gulliksen, Julie Airis, Sharon Hastings, Betty Mann, Myra Murphy, Debbie Sowles, Connie Sparks, Linda Gill, and Georgeanne DeWoody. Your feedback, comments, and corrections were invaluable.

A special thank you to Jim Smoke, author and pastor, who has encouraged me to dream big and write books. Jim, I have learned so much from you and thank the Lord that He brought you here to the desert.

Thank you to Greg Johnson of WordServe Literary Group for encouraging me to pursue the things the Lord places on my heart and for representing me as my agent.

A special thank you to all the pastors, directors of women's ministries, and leaders who are faithfully teaching the Word of God. I am on your team and desire to be one of your greatest cheerleaders. Your faithfulness is such an encouragement to me.

There are not enough words to describe how grateful I am for Harvest House Publishers and their incredible team. I want to especially thank Bob Hawkins Jr. for encouraging me to write the books God has placed on my heart. I will be eternally grateful to the Lord for putting me together with Harvest House. I will never forget the day when I first met you, Bob, along with Steve Miller…what a day that was and the beginning of many exciting things that the Lord is doing. Thank you, Terry Glaspey, for your vision and encouragement; Gene Skinner, for editing my books with such care and discernment; Carolyn McCready, for your encouragement and joy; Barb Sherrill and Katie Lane, for your vision for my books; and so many others including LaRae Weikert, Steve Miller, John Constance, Betty Fletcher, Kimberly Shumate, and Peggy Wright. And finally, thank you to Bob and Shirley Hawkins, for your faithful service to our Lord and for believing in me and encouraging me in the writing of my books. I'll never forget meeting you, Bob. It was a day that changed my life forever. To God be the glory.

Thank you all, and I love you.

ABOUT THE AUTHOR

Catherine Martin is a summa cum laude graduate of Bethel Theological Seminary with a Master of Arts degree in Theological Studies. She is founder and president of Quiet Time Ministries, director of women's ministries at Southwest Community Church in Indian Wells, California, and adjunct faculty member of Biola University. She is the author of *Six Secrets to a Powerful Quiet Time*, *Knowing and Loving the Bible*, and *Walking with the God Who Cares*, published by Harvest House Publishers, and *Pilgrimage of the Heart*, *Revive My Heart!* and *A Heart That Dances*, published by NavPress. She has also written *The Quiet Time Notebook*, *A Heart on Fire*, *A Heart to See Forever*, and *A Heart That Hopes in God*, published by Quiet Time Ministries Press. She is senior editor for *Enriching Your Quiet Time* quarterly magazine. As a popular speaker at retreats and conferences, Catherine challenges others to seek God and love Him with all of their heart, soul, mind, and strength. For more information about Catherine, visit www.quiettime.org, www.catherinemartinonline.com, and www.cathsblog.com.

ABOUT QUIET TIME MINISTRIES

Quiet Time Ministries is a nonprofit organization offering resources for your quiet time. Visit us online at www.quiettime.org. The Quiet Time Ministries Resources and Training Center located in Bermuda Dunes, California, offers conferences and workshops to encourage others in their relationship with the Lord.

Quiet Time Ministries
Post Office Box 14007
Palm Desert, CA 92255
1-800-925-6458
760-772-2357
www.quiettime.org

OTHER *WALKING WITH THE GOD WHO CARES* RESOURCES

available from Quiet Time Ministries

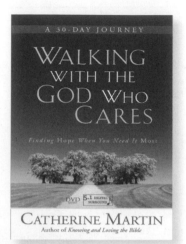

Companion DVD

This Companion DVD with six messages by Catherine Martin is designed to accompany your 30-day journey of *Walking with the God Who Cares*. Each message is filled with inspiration and encouragement and is ideal for individuals or groups. The Companion DVD is available from Quiet Time Ministries online at www.quiettime.org or by phone at 1-800-925-6458.

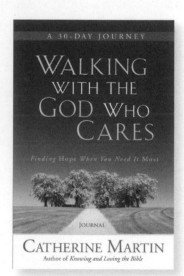

Companion Journal

This Companion Journal is designed for use with your 30-day journey of *Walking with the God Who Cares*. It contains journal and prayer pages taken from the *Quiet Time Notebook* published by Quiet Time Ministries Press. Also included are promise pages to "write a check" on the promise as described in *Walking with the God Who Cares*. These pages will help you learn how to find the promise, embrace the promise, trust the promise, and live the promise. The Companion Journal is available from Quiet Time Ministries online at www.quiettime.org or by phone at 1-800-925-6458.